GOD

WEARS

Lipstick

Kabbalah for Women

Kabbalah Publishing is a registered DBA of
The Kabbalah Centre International, Inc.
155 E. 48th St., New York, NY 10017
1062 S. Robertson Blvd., Los Angeles, CA 90035

1.800.Kabbalah
www.kabbalah.com

First Edition January 2005
First Trade Paperback Edition December 2007
Printed in Canada
ISBN 978-1-57189-581-3

Design: Hyun Min Lee (HL Design) www.hldesignco.com

G O D

W E A R S

Kabbalah for Women

www.kabbalah.com™

K A B B A L I S T   K A R E N   B E R G

Dedication

It is my dream that all the children of the world are given the wisdom for making wise choices, toward lives of certainty, happiness, care for others, and most importantly, control over their destinies.

Every human being contains a spark of God. By extending that awareness throughout the world, we will free ourselves from prejudice, war, and hatred. This planet will at last become what our Creator intended: Heaven on Earth.

Table of Contents

PART II: KABBALISTIC TOOLS

Acknowledgments

First I want to thank the Rav. If it were not for you, for your energy, for your gifts, for your strength, there would be no content for this book. I could not be who I am if you were not so clearly who you are.

And were it not for the work from all of our lifetime together, there would not be this cosmic opportunity to bring this spiritual body of wisdom to the world. With all my love, my darling, thank you.

And thank you to those people who have dedicated their talent and commitment to bringing this wisdom to women. That we may use our Godly power to reveal the Light of the Creator in this generation so that the darkness will fade once and for all. You are as much a part of making this project happen as I. Thank you, Nili Herzog, Jai Collins, Lisa Mirchin, Peter Guzzardi, and Susan Golant, who sculpted my words into form.

INTRODUCTION

I was a wild child who had a crazy childhood.

My father died in 1942, during World War II, right before I was born. Mother was looking to make a life for herself, so I spent most of my time with my grandmother. I was really close to her, and with her help, I raised myself. Eventually my mother married my stepdad, and they had a child together, my stepsister, who is 12 years my junior.

You would think that after this second marriage my life would have settled down, but it didn't. My stepdad was a hotel manager in Miami Beach, Florida, and it was seasonal work. So I would start school in New York, but by November we would be back in Miami. Then we would head back to New York as the weather heated up and the snowbirds fled. And each time we returned, they placed me in a different school. Altogether, I went to 13 different public schools.

It was a nomadic, unstable existence—one in which I never got the protection of a "normal" household or family. And externally, I was a mess. I was five years behind in reading, and my classmates made fun of me. They'd call me "stupid" and "retard." One night some kids threw me into a construction pit. I started crying. I couldn't get out. I was afraid I would die down there.

Why am I telling you all of this? Is it your sympathy I seek? Not at all.

That incident was a turning point in my life. It was the first time I ever felt the presence of God, which came to me as a voice in my head.

"Why are you crying?" it asked. "Don't you understand what's happening? You watch. You'll see. There's a reason for everything that's
come down in your life." I was only ten years old at the time, but since
that moment, I have always known that there was a force greater than
me and my little existence. I was being shaped for the life I would
lead. And since that moment, I've always had that voice inside of me
and have always felt comfortable in places where others have not.

My life then started to improve. At the age of 12, I met a wonderful
teacher, a man who loved me as though I were his daughter. He saw
my potential and took me under his wing. By the time I reached high
school, I'd made English honors.

The spiritual part of my life blossomed long before I got involved with
my husband or with The Kabbalah Centre. Because I sensed the constant presence of God, I started reading everything I could lay my
hands on about energy, spirituality, reincarnation, and astrology. I felt
good in that arena; it was a blessing. I didn't understand fashion (I'm
still a terrible dresser), I hated to go shopping, and eventually I would
become an awful cook and homemaker. The so-called feminine arts
escaped me because that wasn't the role I was meant to play. But I
did know people. My girlfriends used to ask me, "Do you remember
Phyl, the girl in the pink dress with the matching purse and shoes?"
I'd wrack my brain. "You mean the one who doesn't smile?"

It was clear that I was not going to be much interested in the external;
instead, I would turn more to the internal. But not quite yet. When I

first met my future husband, Rav Berg (*Rav* is simply another way of saying "teacher"), I had no idea we were meant for each other. I was 16 at the time and living with my grandma. I needed to support myself because I wanted to finish high school. But I couldn't bear another move to Florida, so I took a job in a business that the Rav owned with his brother-in-law. I worked there for six months. Looking back on it, I am amazed at how oblivious both of us were about what would ultimately take place between us. We were not ready for each other, so the spark just wasn't there. In fact, I disliked the man. He wasn't the Rav yet but was a strong and powerful businessman, and I was a brash, rebellious kid.

I'd answer the office phone.

"Who's calling, please?" I'd ask, cracking my chewing gum.

"Mayor Wagner," the caller replied.

"Yeah, right, and I'm the Pope," I'd say, and I'd hang up. Only it really was the mayor of New York. I'm surprised no one fired me.

At 17, I left the Rav's employ and married a wonderful man. I needed to make a life for myself. I was 18 when our first child, Leah, was born and 19 when her sister Suri arrived. My first husband promised me heaven and earth, and he delivered. Whatever I asked was fine with him. He gave and gave and gave—but at some point, I was surprised to discover that I was unhappy. My husband gave, but I couldn't take.

I wanted something more from life—something that would be fulfilling, that would give me energy. And with him, kind as he was, there was nothing to push against, nowhere to grow.

So I told my husband, "I love you like a brother, and we should be good friends, but I can't stay married to you." Even though our marriage was breaking up, I continued to develop his building contractor business for him, and it did very well. But once I felt he could take care of himself and make it on his own, I left.

Then, eight years after I'd first worked for the Rav, I met him again. I happened to be in need of a secretary, so I decided to contact my former colleague, Carmen. Last I'd heard, she was still working for the Rav and his brother-in-law. So I phoned the office, and Carmen answered. We had a brief conversation, and in passing, I asked, "Is Mr. Berg still involved in the business?"

"No, he's not," Carmen explained. "He moved to Israel, and I see him only occasionally. But when he's in New York, he usually stops by to pick up his mail."

I asked Carmen to say "hi" the next time she saw him, and I hung up. Not ten minutes later, my phone rang. It was the Rav. He had just flown back to New York and happened to walk into Carmen's office only a few moments after she'd finished talking with me.

I felt strangely flustered at the sound of his voice.

"What are you doing these days?" I asked, a little breathlessly.

"Oh, I gave up my business activities," he explained. "I've been studying Kabbalah for the past seven years with my teacher in Israel. My teacher passed away four days ago, so that's why I've come home." I was intrigued. From my readings on reincarnation and astrology, I knew that Kabbalah was the seed of all spiritual teachings. So on an impulse, I asked, "Can I make a deal with you?"

"What kind of deal?" he wanted to know.

"If I come back to work for you at no charge," I blurted, "will you teach me everything you know about Kabbalah?"

"Okay, why not?" he agreed, and we made a date for dinner that night to discuss the details. I have to tell you, at that meeting, it was all over. We knew instantly that we were meant for each other.

A week later, we met again, this time for breakfast at Ratner's restaurant on New York's Lower East Side. But the Rav did not look happy this time. In fact, he seemed positively downcast. Instead of talking about himself, he asked me, "How've you been?"

"Fine," I said, "but I have to tell you, I had the wildest dream last night."

He nodded as if to say, "Go on."

"A man whom I've never met came to me in my dream," I began. "And when I turned and looked at him, he put his hands over my head. He said something to me in what sounded like Hebrew, but I didn't understand him. Then he turned to leave. I tried to grab his coat and ask him what he was saying, but he just walked away." This was all the more bizarre, I explained, because as a fourth-generation American Jew from a relatively assimilated family, I'd never had a Jewish education or learned Hebrew.

But rather than being disturbed by my weird dream, the Rav perked up. "Describe this man," he said, his face flushing with excitement. Fortunately, I was able to do so in detail, because the image had been quite vivid. "He was dressed in a long coat and carried a cane," I explained. "And he had a big fur hat on his head."

The Rav became elated. "Before going to sleep last night," he replied, "I asked my teacher to come to me and let me know if it was right for me to teach you. But he never showed up, so I arrived here this morning with a heavy heart. I thought I'd have to tell you that our deal was off. But the man you describe in your dream was my teacher. He appeared to you instead of me. And even more important, he has clearly given his blessing."

That was the beginning of our road together. In fact, not long afterward, we decided to get married. But when I went to my mother with the news, she took one look at his picture and said, "You're crazy. What can he give you? What can he offer?" I must say, we did make an unusual pair—the original Odd Couple. He was an Orthodox Jew in a long black frock coat and a big black fur hat, and I was a miniskirted, divorced woman in my 20s with two little girls.

With my first husband, I'd had everything that I wanted: the big house, the fancy car, you name it—that is, if you call "everything I wanted" having. But I didn't. I decided that this man and what he had to offer— a life studying the Kabbalah—was what I really wanted.

So I traded the house, the car, and the alimony payments for a tiny apartment in Brooklyn. and a welfare check. My mother said, "You're crazy. How can you give all of this away?" I remember when we first got married, the Rav had to borrow $25 so we could make a Sabbath meal. Still, those were the best years of our lives. At the same time, I won't pretend they were easy. We still came from two different worlds.

In fact, right after we got married, the Rav threw out all of my books on astrology and spirituality—just threw them out. I was so annoyed. And he would go crazy over things that seemed like nonsense to me. Once, he went to the *mikvah*—the ritual bath—to cleanse himself before the Sabbath. But after this ritual, a woman touched his hand by accident, and he hit the roof.

We even fought over a television set. We didn't have a TV, so one day I brought one home. The Rav stood inside the doorway and pushed it out as if it were a smelly dead cat. I ran outside to retrieve it, and he closed the door behind me. So I took the TV and left him in the apartment with my two kids.

When I finally called him, he asked, "You're leaving me? Because of a TV? It's a stupidity."

"That's right," I retorted, "it is a stupidity." So I came home with the TV in tow, and it stayed.

But it was still tough. In fact, I got so fed up with his religiosity that one day I took that big black fur hat off his head and threw it right out the window. I said to him, "Let's understand something. I joined your world, so you've got to come to mine. I can't live with this kind of strictness."

Yet despite our troubles, the Rav and I didn't give up on our commitment to each other. Although the merging of our two worlds was difficult, our love and shared desire to create something bigger than ourselves prevailed. In fact, it was our differences that eventually made it possible to have a Kabbalah that is accessible to everyone.

Shortly thereafter, we moved to Israel with my two children. I truly didn't want to go, but I knew that it meant a lot to the Rav for his personal growth, and he felt that our children would benefit from it. Because of this, I agreed to the move. So we started a new life in a foreign country with only $4000 to our name. I didn't speak Hebrew, and we had no family or friends there. And by that time our two boys had been born, so we were now a family of six.

At that time, few people knew anything about Rav Berg or, for that matter, about Kabbalah. We were just beginning to find our direction. We knew we wanted to have a lasting spiritual effect on mankind and believed that Kabbalah was the way to achieve that goal, but we lacked help and money. However, our scant means and uncomplicated lives proved to be one of our greatest blessings. With no friends or extended family around us and nothing to distract us, we had all the time in the world to study and to love our children. We would take our kids to the park and play with them every day. And each night, when we all went to bed, we would sing songs, and the Rav would tell the children stories about a horse named Silver and the imaginary farm where he lived.

And I began to study. In fact, much of what you'll find in this book is a result of my years of delving into the knowledge contained in the Kabbalah. But again, it wasn't easy. For centuries, Kabbalah had been accessible only to scholarly Jewish men over the age of 40 and had been forbidden to all others, including women. In fact, it was thought that the study of Kabbalah would drive one to madness, and many kabbalists were tortured or killed for their efforts.

This tradition of secrecy passed through generation after generation of male kabbalists until 1968, when Rav Berg first became director of The Kabbalah Centre in Tel Aviv. At this time, he was studying the Ten Luminous Emanations with his teacher. Those teachings provide a deep understanding of the "big picture" of life—how the world came to be, the nature of God, why we are here, and how man was formed in that context.

But it was all so abstract. As you start to understand the kabbalistic nature of women and men that I will convey in these pages, you will begin to appreciate why the Rav was more involved with the theoretical wisdom and why it took me, a woman, to give that wisdom a form and a structure that would make it available to all people. Indeed, it took a woman to knock on the door and say, "Bring it to a format. Make it real."

So I asked the Rav, "What about a person who is unhappy or who has a certain kind of karma or was born under a particular sign? If everything happens for a reason, then issues like astrology, reincarnation, and past-life experience, which I know to be true, must be included in your books somewhere. If kabbalistic teachings really have a truth, then they must incorporate these experiences as well."

This prompted the Rav to start looking and studying more. In the writings of Rav Isaac Luria, the famed 16th-century Spanish Kabbalist who is also known as the Ari (the Lion), he found *The Gates of Reincarnation*. And in *The Book of Formation*—the first recorded document of Kabbalah, written some 4000 years ago by the Patriarch Abraham—he found a whole universe of astrology. We soon began studying this wisdom together.

Finally I said, "Look, if I can understand these teachings (and I'm not such a great big soul), then others can too. Let's open The Kabbalah Centre to everyone."

"How do you want to give the classes?" the Rav asked me.

"Men and women together."

"What?" he responded. The thought of women learning Kabbalah was hard enough, but women learning together with men? That was unheard of. "Forget about it." he shot back.

"What can happen?" I asked.

"Women. We'll get murdered," he said.

But I've been rebellious and stubborn all my life, so I insisted on opening the wisdom of Kabbalah to everyone, regardless of race, gender, or religious belief. When we are on a spiritual path, we are seeking to reconnect with Spirit—the Light of the Creator. This spirit has no name—it is not Christian, Jewish, or Buddhist; it is not male or female; it is not limited in any way. It is just Spirit, existing far beyond the confines of any particular faith. And it has no gender. If I could do it, other women should be able to connect to its wisdom as well.

Yet it wasn't easy to open the teachings of Kabbalah to the whole world. Historically, Kabbalah had been reserved only for the most advanced scholars. By making it available to anyone who was interested in it, we were defying a 4000-year-old tradition. But despite our difficulties, the study of Kabbalah has become more and more popular, and The Kabbalah Centre has grown from a small, exclusive organization based in Israel into a worldwide entity whose 50 branches have provided instruction to nearly four million students.

And I believe that the heart of our success lies in the understanding that God is part of each human being. Whatever a person's faith may be, it is developed with tools that I'll share with you in this book. Those tools will enhance your everyday life, but not because God will strike you dead if you don't use them. The tools are there for you, for me, for all of us. God doesn't need them. And from them we should draw pleasure, which is the purpose of our existence here on earth.

* * *

I have written *God Wears Lipstick*, the first Kabbalistic Bible for women, to help you become aware that you don't have to be a 40-year-old man—and a Talmud scholar to boot—to learn Kabbalah. You can be a female in your 20s or in your 70s. You can be a Christian or a Moslem. You can be a full-time mother or a high-powered executive, a movie star or a sales clerk. And however much knowledge this book will bring you, it will give you the nourishment to go further and become as great as you can be in your potential spiritual enlightenment.

You may know about a tradition in Judaism in which women light and bless candles on Friday night at the dinner table to usher in the Sabbath. This is a deeply meaningful act. It is the female who brings the Light into the home, and it is the female who manifests all the energy and puts it in its place, helping others grow. Women are the nourishers of the world, and as such, we are the messengers of God. Without the vessel, there cannot be Light—it does not exist in a void.

You share that very important role, and in *God Wears Lipstick*, I hope to help you manifest it.

Are you ready?

PART I

KABBALISTIC

WISDOM

1

We Have Desires

So many desires.

We all want to understand ourselves better, to live more fulfilling lives, to have a richer experience of who we are and what we are here to contribute. All of us want to be happy. And in truth, most of us really want the same things out of life: We want to love and be loved; we want to have satisfying relationships; we want to enjoy financial security; we want full bellies and slim waistlines; we want our children to be happy and safe.

We want success, we want to eat chocolate, we want to party, we want to sit and contemplate, we want sex, we want companionship, we want safety, we want babies, we want a great new novel to read, we want the perfect lipstick, we want a good man who is our soul-mate, we want world peace, we want to learn, we want to be left alone, we want to dance, we want an ice-cold soda, we want a dozen red roses, we want to swim in the ocean, we want to hike in the mountains, we want to hide under the covers, we want those diamond earrings and Jimmy Choo shoes, we want to share, we want to love. We want and want and want.

And we have questions—so many questions.

Deep down, we all crave to understand the meaning of our lives. Perhaps as a child you might have wondered, "Why was I born? What is the purpose of my life?" But soon we all grew up and got busy. We had to pay the rent, make sure the kids were dressed for school, pick up the groceries, tend to the marriage, chauffeur the soccer team, and pursue our careers. So out of exhaustion, we simply stopped asking the profound questions that once fascinated us as children. But do we have to? Don't you continue to wonder, *Why was I created?*

In *God Wears Lipstick*, I aim to reveal to you what Kabbalah explains about what life is really supposed to be like. Why we are here. Why things happen the way they do. Where you got your brain, your thoughts, your desires, your emotions, the people you know, and the talents you possess. How all of this fits into the larger picture of the universe, and how you can find lasting fulfillment. These are the spiritual rules of the game of life.

What would happen if you were to learn them? *All of your potential would be actualized.* In fact, the whole purpose of the study of Kabbalah is to enlighten you about these nonphysical laws for the sake of your receiving fulfillment.

But what is *spiritual?* The word means many different things to many different people. For now, anything beyond what your five senses can perceive—if you can't see it, taste it, smell it, feel it, or hear it—can be regarded as spiritual. In the past you might have used words such as *emotional*, *intuitive*, or *gut feeling*. "I have a good feeling about that person," you might have said. Or "Yuck. He makes my skin crawl." These are reactions that you can't identify using your senses, so let's call them spiritual.

The word *Kabbalah* comes from the phrase *to receive*. Kabbalah is all about learning *how to receive* the fulfillment you are seeking. And that will lead to true, long-lasting, permanent success in your life. So where do we begin? Where else, if not before the beginning.

2

Before the Beginning

Why you are here today and who you are—the makeup you're wearing, or the way you dress or smile, look at a man, or cuddle your baby—are all a reflection of *why you are here at all*. And Kabbalah explains to us that we have to go back—all the way back, to before the time of creation—to understand that gigantic question.

Before the beginning, in what Kabbalah calls the Endless World, two forces allowed creation.

One force is called the Light. This is the infinite, constant desire to share. The Light is all good. It is the energy of the universe—the nonphysical energy we are all looking for—but it's energy that has intelligence. The Light is the universal energy that exists within everything—in rocks, trees, and taxicabs; in dogs and desks; and even in your mother-in-law. *It is the Light Force of the Creator*—the Light of God. Sharing is actually that energy—God's energy.

In fact, the ancient kabbalists define the force called God as infinite power of giving, infinite energy of imparting, of fulfillment. What kind of fulfillment? It is the energy of peace and the energy of clarity; the energy of health and financial abundance; the energy of affirmation and love and relationships; the energy of every blessing you hope for. In fact, when we use the word *Light* in the world of Kabbalah, we mean everything you can possibly imagine that is wonderful: self-confidence, happiness, fulfillment, love, creativity, abundance, security, respect, joy, health. You name it—if it's good, it's the Light.

The purpose of studying Kabbalah is to learn how to plug into the Light and receive all of its blessings. Kabbalah helps us understand that we can glean the Light from everything, even from a tablecloth. In fact, the moment you accept that your being, who you are, is the flow of Light, and the moment you tune into that flow, everything around you will be illuminated.

The Endless Light is amazing. It shares and shares and shares. Imagine it as a plus, the ultimate positive. The utter and complete giver of life, of warmth, of happiness.

THE VESSEL

The Light is pure sharing, but it needed something on which to bestow its beneficence. It needed to create an entity whose capacity was so vast that it could receive, continuously and endlessly, all that the Light had to give. So the Light, which is the infinite energy of giving, created an infinite receiver. In Kabbalah, we call this the original soul or the original Vessel. If the Light is a plus, then the Vessel is a minus—the second force of creation.

Why did the kabbalists use the word *Vessel*? In the same way that a cup holds water, each of us is a container that has the capacity to receive what the Creator has in store for us—all the Light, all the energy, all the fulfillment that we are looking for. The original vessel is the original soul, the original receiver, the original being that was created for the sake of receiving all the pleasures and goodness that the Creator and the Light wanted to give us.

In kabbalistic terms, we say that the Light is the *cause* and the Vessel is the *effect*. The Vessel is the effect of the Light's desire to share. The Vessel just wants everything you could ever think of, everything the Light has to offer, every form of desire—to be happy, to be famous, to be loved, to sleep, to eat, to dance, those diamond earrings and Jimmy Choo shoes. Everything exists in the infinite desire to receive.

And for a while, there was complete harmony. The sharing nature was sharing: The Light gave, and the receiving nature was receiving, so the Vessel got. And it was perfect.

TROUBLE IN PARADISE

But then things changed.

In any creation, you find the essence of its creator. When you marvel at a work of art, for instance, you know it's a Renoir or a Rembrandt because the painter is in his painting. The same holds true of the

Vessel and the Light in the Endless World. Although the nature of the Vessel is only to receive, upon being imbued with the outpouring of love from the Creator, the Vessel also absorbed the Light's sharing nature.

This was a problem for the Vessel, because simply continuing to receive was no longer fulfilling. And so it developed a new desire. It said, "You know what? I'm not happy just receiving. To be fulfilled, I need to be like you. I need to give and share too."

So what, exactly, is this need to share?

I was in that situation with my first husband. He was so good to me— all he wanted to do was give and give. But there was no room for me to give back to him, and after a while I became restless and unhappy. You might experience a similar dilemma with a good friend. Imagine that she is constantly inviting you out to dinner and a movie. But every time you go out, she pays. Do you feel good about it? Of course not. It bothers you. You want to pay, too. Even if you know that her generosity is born of a pure love for you—in fact, especially if this is the case—you'll look for ways to give back. If that cannot be done materially, then you'll look for some other ways to reciprocate. And if you can't find any, pretty soon you'll simply decline her invitations. It's just too uncomfortable to be constantly on the receiving end.

In fact, this is one of the ground rules of Kabbalah: If you receive anything in this world, you're conditioned to share. And it's not a condition that philosophers deal with; it's a condition that's in the nature, the very DNA of the universe.

This desire to share is exactly what happened to the Vessel. It said, "I'm receiving, receiving, receiving, but I'm doing nothing for it. That makes me really uneasy. I want to share, too. Let me give something back to you, Light."

But now there was a problem. The Light, as you recall, is only about giving. It doesn't have the capacity to receive; that capacity is just not there. So the Light said to the Vessel, "I cannot take anything from you."

"But there is no way I'm going to continue to receive without sharing," the Vessel responded.

And so it was that our world came about from an impasse.

3

So What Happened?

The Big Bang.

Our universe came about as a result of the Vessel saying, "I feel ashamed. I'm getting something for nothing. In kabbalistic terms, this is called *Bread of Shame*; I want the opportunity to share as well." In the Endless World, the original Vessel had everything except the chance to actually earn the Light it was receiving.

So what did the Vessel do? It pushed back and resisted the Light. It said to the Light, "STOP. NO MORE."

Since the Creator's only intention was to please the Vessel, the Creator withdrew the Light. In Kabbalah, we say that it *restricted* itself. It constricted into a single finite point. And at that moment there was such utter darkness, it was unbearable for the Vessel. So the Light rushed back in at full force. But the Vessel wasn't ready—it hadn't transformed its nature. So at that instant, it lost its original wholeness and was shattered, exploding into an infinite number of fragments— thus creating all the souls of mankind as well as time, space, motion, and the physical universe as we know it today.

Here's how modern scientists describe the event:

> Approximately 15 billion years ago, before the universe came into existence, there was nothing. No time. No space. The universe began in a single point. This point was surrounded by nothingness. It had no width. No depth. No length. This speck contained the whole of space, time, and matter. The point erupted in an explosion of unimaginable force, expanding at the speed of light. This energy eventually cooled and coalesced into matter—stars, galaxies, and planets.

The Big Bang.

This shattering of the original Vessel created our world. In fact, the Creator brought this physical universe into being to fulfill the Vessel's desire to share. The Vessel is the consummate soul. Our real purpose in this world is to learn to become a giver, the Light, a cause—one in which we seek to fulfill our desires and yearn to feel once again the Light and love of the Creator.

For every human being, life thus became a process of reconnecting to the Light Force of the Creator so that we might regain our former wholeness. However, the intention was not that we simply return to our original state. This physical world was created in order to give us an opportunity that we did not have in the Endless World—to become beings of sharing, like our Creator, and not just passive receivers. In fact, learning to share unconditionally is the purpose of the physical realm and is the only way we can taste of the bounty of the Creator. The purpose of Creation is to give us a chance to reconnect with the original circuitry of love and thus reunite with the Creator, who is the source of all that is good and whole. We do this by learning how to share with others so that we become like the Creator.

4

Two Parallel Systems

Two parallel forces exist in the universe: Light and Vessel, sun and moon, positive and negative, sharing and receiving, yin and yang, male and female. And everything in this world operates from these two parallel forces.

Consider for a minute the sun and the moon. In the beginning, when days were first created, the fourth day of creation—the center of the week—was Wednesday. It was on this day that the sun and moon were created. But they weren't equal. Each orb was imbued with a particular energy—and as we all know, one has less than the other. The moon is variable and emits no Light of its own, but merely reflects the sun's constant outpouring of Light.

A battle immediately ensued over who would reign. The moon wanted the same Light as the sun. These two powerful forces began vying for the energy.

So how was this conflict resolved?

The Creator insisted, "There can't be two kings under one crown." The Creator said to the sun, "You will have *your* time, but not for always." And then the Creator turned to the moon and said, "And you will have your time." So on the fourth day of creation, it was decided that until the coming of the Messiah, the Age of Aquarius, the sun—the male energy—would rule over the moon, which is female. Until that time, the moon would remain a Vessel, reflecting the sun's light.

The sun and the moon, the Light and the Vessel, male and female. According to Kabbalah, the male represents endless sharing: the Light—while the female represents receiving: the Vessel.

Perhaps you might jump in here and say, "Hey, that's not fair. Why should men be the Light and women only the Vessel?" For some reason, we have come to believe that we actually want all of the Light's attributes. But imagine that you're dying of thirst. Now visualize a pipe that's gushing water. Water, water everywhere, but there's no basin or cup to catch it in; the only container you can find is a bottomless bowl. What is the value of this outpouring of good if the parallel system—the Vessel—is not there to hold it and determine how much water is collected? The water is just there, flowing. The same can be said of electricity in our walls. You have pure energy, in all of its abundance, flowing through the wires—but with no lamp and bulb, there's no light. *Light needs a Vessel to give it shape and form.*

I recently had a real-life experience with this concept when an electrician came to my house to install some new fixtures. We talked about what would be most effective, and he suggested sconces that shot light against the wall directly up to the ceiling.

"But will that give us enough light?" I wanted to know.

Do you know what he told me? "We can't see the light unless it hits a surface that reflects it back to us." The wall, in this case, would be the light's vessel. My electrician couldn't have been more kabbalistic if he had tried.

Now consider my conversation with the Rav about bringing Kabbalah into an accessible format. The Rav was more involved with theoretical wisdom—abstract information. He was imagining the universe and flow of energy. He listened. He learned. "But what about the practical application of that knowledge?" I kept asking. "My life. Now. What does it all mean? Don't talk to me about philosophy. Tell me whether I should wake up on the right or the left side of the bed tomorrow." I demanded that he give all that free-flowing wisdom a form and a structure so as to make it available to all people. This is the role of women in relation to men.

This concept, in a more perverse way, also reminds me of Laban's story in *The Bible*. Laban was the brother of Rebecca and the father of Rachel and Leah. But he was evil—selfish, greedy, and duplicitous. He was your basic lying, cheating scoundrel, especially when it came to dealing with his son-in-law, Jacob. Like all others, he too possessed a transcendental white Light, but his was not contained within a Vessel—no wife was mentioned in *The Bible* in relation to him. Instead, Laban's energy flew in all directions without a purpose. He became self-destructive because he lacked the Vessel that would shape his energy toward a worthy goal.

Think about how these principles might be operating in your own life with your partner.

MALE AND FEMALE

There had to be two forces, two creations in the Endless World. But *The Zohar*—the main body of the teachings of Kabbalah, revealed some 2000 years ago in Israel by Rav Shimon bar Yochai—teaches us *as above, so below*. What existed in the Endless World also exists on earth. Light is a masculine force and the Vessel a feminine one, and this principle manifests in humanity as well as in the animal and vegetable kingdoms. In fact, men and women were created as part of this same system—they are only one aspect of those two parallel universes, two parallel forces.

In Kabbalah, we refer to the masculine as *Zeir Anpin* and the feminine as *Malchut*. These are kabbalistic code names, *Zeir Anpin* being the plus, the sharer, the masculine energy, and *Malchut* meaning the minus, the receiver, the feminine energy. I will relate to women in this book as *Malchut*.

Malchut means a recipient, a Vessel. This physical world, our kingdom, is *Malchut*—the glass, the table, the buildings, the earth, the moon, the body. These are all part of the world of *Malchut* because they have physicality. But what creates or brings power into a glass or a table or a body? It's the thought, the energy, the soul within them. That would be *Zeir Anpin*, which means the Light. We know, based on science, that we humans use only five percent of our potential. We harness our senses to help us understand our physical world of *Malchut*, but our senses do not give us an accurate or complete picture of what reality is. There's a whole realm for which we have no tools, understanding, or ability to perceive with our senses, yet that realm—the world of *Zeir Anpin*—exists nonetheless, and in so many ways.

For instance, these two parallel systems are represented by the egg and the sperm, the egg being a Vessel. The egg is the home where the sperm can grow and develop. In fertility work, we know that doctors can freeze the sperm and the embryo, but they can never freeze the egg. They just can't. When you put the male and female, the plus and the minus together, there is no higher form of creation in this world than a child, a new life. Nothing can imitate it.

The two systems are also represented by heaven and earth. Heaven is the sharer and earth the receiver. Now, does that make one more important than the other? Of course not. In fact, you can't have one without the other. We understand kabbalistically that the earth is grown and seeded by the rain—that nourishment is male energy because the sun and water can provide for an entire field, not just a single point. In the same way, a man can sire many children in only a few days, but a woman will usually bear only one child at a time.

The two systems are also represented by the soul and the body. The masculine represents the soul, while the feminine represents the body. No wonder we have a need for massages, manicured nails, hair-stylists, and lovely clothes. None of this is negative. One of the elements that determines how much Light you can receive is the quality of your Vessel, so as a woman, you have a need to beautify that Vessel. Consider what happens when you buy a bouquet of red roses for your home. You would never think to put them in a cardboard box, would you? Instead, you would consider the beauty of the vase as much as you would the freshness of the flowers.

It's no coincidence that males and females are different. We operate in two parallel systems that work simultaneously. Our two genders are just another aspect of the way this universe is structured (which explains why there are not three, five, or nine genders). Male represents the ability to share energy. But the capsule, the Vessel that feeds that energy and manifests it, making it grow and come to fruition, is female. You need Light to have a Vessel and a Vessel to manifest Light. Everything we see in our physical world has a spiritual essence. Once the Light, the spiritual essence, the energy is taken out of the Vessel, it dies. The soul leaves.

But how do you bring these two parallel forces together?

5

The Light Bulb Principle

Mankind. We were created to unify these two parallel systems. In fact, the connection between them is created by human behavior—by combining the desire to receive with the desire to share.

The best way to understand this is to use the metaphor of a light bulb.

EDISON'S DISCOVERY

The Zohar teaches us, *as above, so below*. This means that the physical laws of our universe, like gravity, come from somewhere—they weren't invented but have existed from the beginning of time. In fact, we can understand the simple laws of electricity as a representation of the spiritual Light of the Creator. But first, let's study the laws that allow a light bulb to shine.

Take a close look at any old-fashioned screw-in light bulb (not the halogen or fluorescent variety) and you'll see two poles—a plus or positive and a minus or negative—along with a delicate filament or wire that connects the two. The positive pole provides the energy; it's the source. The negative pole attracts and draws the energy; it's the recipient.

Logically, you might think, "Plus, minus; give, take—it's done." But the light bulb doesn't work that way. If you connect the positive pole directly to the negative one, you may get a short circuit and perhaps even a healthy shock, or the electricity will just continue to flow on through but shed no light.

The amazing thing that Edison discovered was that you need a filament that actually *resists* the energy flowing through it from the positive to the negative pole. The resistance, the push-back, is what creates the light. The moment Edison inserted a filament that bounced some of the electricity back toward the positive pole, the light revealed itself.

And what's the difference between a 10-watt bulb and a 100-watt bulb? That's easy. It's the amount of resistance the filament puts up. The filament in a 100-watt bulb resists more than the filament in a bulb with less wattage, and so the lamp glows more brightly. The opposite, of course, would be true of a "dim bulb".

Kabbalah calls the filament the third or central column (the left column being the negative and the right being the positive), and this will be of great importance to us as we go forward.

Now imagine that the filament becomes tired and says, "You know what? I'm done. Just bring it on. Go on through me; I can't resist it anymore." What happens in the bulb? A bright flash of light and then darkness. Nothing. The void. We say that the light bulb is dead.

Now think of the electrical wires buried within the walls of your home. What determines how much electricity is going to be revealed? The same power is traveling in those wires, so what controls how much of it will be used? You might use a bulb or a toaster oven or a computer or a washing machine—but again, the answer is simple. Whatever equipment you are using will determine how much electricity will be drawn. And if there's no equipment, the electricity will flow uselessly. A room without a lamp will be dark even if there's electricity in the walls. And what is the equipment? The Vessel. The two parallel systems need each other in order to activate one another's force, which is ultimately the force of fulfillment.

TURNING ON THE LIGHT BULB

So let's relate the laws of the light bulb to our lives.

What is the minus—the negative pole that draws the current, the "I want"? As with the original Vessel, it is our Desire to Receive, the natural tendency that motivates each of us to seek fulfillment and joy. Whether you're looking for some security, for some help, for some love, for some success, for an address, for a relationship, for sex, for drugs, for energy, for support, for recognition, for beauty, or for good feelings about yourself, you're operating out of that basic Desire to Receive.

Our Vessel, our desire, determines how much Light or how many good things appear in our lives. In fact, the amount of energy a home will have is governed by the female, the wife. She is the Light of that house, and the capacity of her Vessel sets the limit for the Light that will come into her home.

In Kabbalah, the motivating power that moves us to pour ourselves a glass of water or buy a new car is called left-column energy, or the Desire to Receive. The great Kabbalist Rav Ashlag once wrote that we humans would not twitch a single finger were it not for some inner desire. Our desire is our Vessel—the empty cup that constantly seeks to be filled. There is no limit to our desire.

Our Desire to Receive is also called "the negative," but not in a pejorative way. This refers to our natural motivation to accomplish tasks, to get things in life. In the atom, which is the building block of physical matter, the negative is represented by the electron.

So what's on the right?

Why, giving, of course. It's the flowing current, the source, the sharing nature of the Light of the Creator.

We are all fascinated by this energy. If you're attracted to another person—or, for that matter, to money, wisdom, recognition, or even a new outfit—what are you looking for? What do all of those things represent? Energy, pure and simple. You are attracted to a dress or a person or a music CD because it's a channel that transmits some energy to you. When you acquire it, you feel good—for a while, anyway.

We all like to be filled with the strength and energy of fulfillment that in Kabbalah we call the plus, the right column, or "the positive." Again, no value judgment is being made here. Right column or "positive" simply means the Desire to Share.

So the negative is our Desire to Receive, and the positive is the energy we're attracted to, the Desire to Share. The energy of receiving and the energy of sharing manifest themselves in many different ways. If your Desire to Receive is for financial success, the energy of financial success will manifest itself as money. The same holds true of sex or love or attention or any other energy source.

THE NATURE OF ENERGY

All energy is good because there's only one source for it. And what is that? The Light of the Creator, of course. There are no other batteries in this world. But the manner in which we receive the Light will determine if that energy will manifest itself as a short circuit or as a lasting current of fulfillment.

White and black energy are the same; the only difference lies in their application. Imagine a powerful individual. If he directs his energy into dismantling companies, destroying people, corrupting values, cheating customers and stockholders, and uprooting families—if, like Laban, he behaves with no scruples—he exhibits black energy. Unfortunately, such a person's energy is often misplaced because he had little nurturing from childhood. He lives in a kill-or-be-killed universe. Think of someone like billionaire Howard Hughes. He had a huge amount of money but died alone of syphilis. But that same person could also be a philanthropist. Like Bill Gates, he could create abundance, bestow large gifts of charity, bring up new people, and create a system that helps humanity. The energy is the same. The difference lies in how it is directed.

A person who takes drugs also draws energy—a tremendous amount of energy. Is the energy itself bad? Not at all. But the way that person receives and interacts with it creates negative results.

Energy is energy. When it's put into a Vessel that doesn't have an uplifting purpose or goal, it becomes black. When it's put into a Vessel that does, it becomes white.

So how can you and I create that white Vessel?

6

We Join the Resistance

Let's go back to our three columns, or the three energy-intelligences within the light bulb. The one on the left is receiving. The one on the right is giving. So what's the middle force? It's *restriction*—the power to resist the immediate flow of energy that goes from the plus to the minus. That's what reveals the Light.

According to Kabbalah, the only way to fulfillment is to be part of this three-column system, in which you have a chance to transform your Desire to Receive for the Self Alone—the gravitational pull to "me, me, me"—into the Desire to Receive for the Sake of Sharing.

The laws of the universe are simple. Every time you receive energy for yourself alone—every time you greedily grab energy without applying restriction, without taking charge of your Desire to Receive, without giving something in return—you partake of Bread of Shame. You will receive the energy, and it will fill you up for a second, creating the rush you crave—but it will then short circuit, and in place of joy, you will find negativity and chaos in your life.

This is a basic law of nature, just like the laws of gravity. This world is designed so that we share whatever it is that we receive. Bill Gates and his wife, for instance, put this sharing to work on a large scale by establishing a philanthropic foundation to distribute their vast wealth and, in smaller ways, by creating a home and having children.

In kabbalistic terms, to restrict means to receive for the sake of sharing with others and not for the self alone. And being spiritual means you're there for other human beings when they need you. You're prepared to leave your comfort zone to help them. That's when the Light of the Creator can flow through you and create miracles for you.

So what does this mean in practical, everyday terms?

- "I want something, so first I have to give."

- "I want people to listen to me, so I need to listen to others."

- "I want to be respected, so I need to give respect."

- "I want to be loved, so I need to give love."

When you worry only about yourself, the Creator can't come in. After all, someone is already looking after you. Only when you worry about others does the Creator see your need.

PROACTIVE VERSUS REACTIVE

In the Endless World, the original Vessel had everything except the opportunity to earn the Light it was receiving. It was mired in Bread of Shame, so like the light bulb filament we described earlier, it resisted the flow of Light and pushed back. It said to the Light Force of the Creator, "Stop. I don't want any more until I can give something back."

When you are proactive—when you push back and resist the Desire to Receive for the Self Alone—you emulate this process of creation.

But certain situations can come to you in life that push your buttons and cause you to say, "Yeah? Well, what about me?" As soon as you start feeling entitled, you become not a cause, not part of the Light, but reactive to it—an effect.

Think about your life. When you indulge in instant gratification and self-ishness, when you fail to make an effort, when you're not initiating energy or taking responsibility, when you just flow with your natural tendency and the easy urge, when you're lazy or you procrastinate—at that moment, are you acting like the Light? Of course not. In fact, in Kabbalah we would say that you're disconnected from the Light. You're behaving from the Desire to Receive for the Self Alone—it's all about "me, me, me."

What does this bring to your life? Chaos and darkness.

The purpose of this physical world is to take you out of the two columns of giving and receiving and, through free will, create the third column. This third column represents the idea of being proactive, and it's not physical. It's a matter of consciousness. It's like the filament—the resistance. Your consciousness helps determine how much Light your Vessel can handle. If your consciousness is all about "me, me, me," then your ability to receive the Light, your Vessel, will be quite small. It's big enough for only one. But if you're thinking about caring for the whole planet, just imagine how big your Vessel can be. That kind of consciousness changes lives. It heals people and allows them to experience true fulfillment.

So perhaps you're asking yourself, "How can I change my situation to be in the Light?"

Again, the answer is easy. The only way to restore the Light, to remove the chaos, and to bring fulfillment is by acting like the Light. That means giving and creating. The Light is not a receiver; the Light is just a giver. And being a creator means being the cause, being the initiator, being *proactive*.

But being a giver and a creator can be hard. It may go against your natural inclination to be *reactive*, to be an effect, to be on the receiving end. Being proactive means resisting temptations and your baser urges—pushing back on the easy money, the something-for-nothing mentality, the unconscious emotion, the ego. Being proactive means taking responsibility rather than living in a victim mentality and end-lessly complaining that the world doesn't treat you right.

Imagine, for example, that you come home from work after a tough day, hungry and tired. The kids are crying for attention, and your hus-band is as exhausted as you are. His socks and underwear clutter the bedroom floor, and toys are strewn about the kitchen. The mail is pil-ing up. The pot is boiling over in more ways than one. What is the reac-tive thing to do? You lose it. You yell and scream and carry on, adding to the chaos. That's the easy road.

If you're coming from a victim mentality, you can do nothing about your situation except complain. If you're coming from a place of expec-tations, you're just building a file against your husband that you add to day after day (much to the detriment of your marriage), and you take no responsibility. In either case, you're being reactive, an effect—and from that place, fulfillment looks like a far-off dream.

But there is a way out of this morass. Recently, the International Institute of Aging researched happy people around the world and found a common thread among them: They all said that they had the power to take control over their lives, to be a cause. When you live in a state that encompasses restriction and proactive behavior, that's where fulfillment and control of the physical universe lies.

So you want a peaceful household when you come home? You want to make sure you're feeling sane? If you don't have expectations that someone else will solve the problem—if you take responsibility for it and become proactive rather than reactive—you'll find 150 creative ways to make your life better. Maybe you'll bring in a nanny from 5 to 7 each evening to cook dinner and ease your transition. Or you'll eat out or call in for Chinese food twice a week. Or you'll ask a neighbor to help out or hire a babysitter and take a breather with your honey.

I recently met a young woman at The Kabbalah Centre in New York who had been a drug addict for five years. But after taking only six classes at The Centre, she never touched drugs again. Never. The end. How? Did she go through drug rehab? Not at all. One day she just decided, "No more drugs." And that was that. She realized that she was dependent on drugs as a way to fulfill her. "I didn't want to be ful-filled by temporary things anymore," she told me, "because after-wards I'd always feel down again. And each time, I'd sink deeper. So I decided to change that. I wanted to change my consciousness, to cre-ate my own fulfillment instead of depending on drugs to do it for me."

Did this change take work from her? Of course it did. Was it effort-less? Of course not. But consciousness made all the difference. Proactive behaviors don't come naturally; you have to invest in them. You have to notice how you're reacting and then engage in proactive behaviors in order to feel happy. You have to have a vision; you have to step beyond your boundaries; you have to take charge of your life. The moment you take responsibility, you realize that you've created a new reality. You can take control; you can change your life. But taking responsibility can be a scary proposition. Most of us would rather cast blame. We'd rather say, "You know what? There's nothing I can do about it." If you discover that you can have some impact, it means you have to step up to the plate and change your life.

We are the only ones who limit ourselves. Our own reactive consciousness gets in the way. When you are ready to let go of your reactive consciousness, you'll have a bigger spiritual desire because you'll be open to receiving all the Light that exists in the universe.

7

But There's a Catch

Okay, so now you can see how the Light and resistance and consciousness might work in your life. But here's the rub.

Back in the Endless World, the two forces of sharing and receiving were almost equal, but there was a problem. The Light was endless Desire to Share. That's the only thing the Light knew how to do. The Vessel received from the Light. Also good, since it embodied the endless Desire to Receive. But what did it receive from the Light? Along with all other good and wonderful things, it received the Desire to Share.

Bringing this down to our earthly concerns, it becomes clear that the male aspect (or the plus or the Light) is a relatively free experience. A man has a singular energy. He is just sharing. This can seem so powerful to us. But remember, male energy is abstract, unformed, and unfocused, just like electricity flowing in the wall without a bulb or an appliance to give it structure.

And what about women? We want to have it all. We represent that aspect called the Vessel—desire. The woman says, "I want, and I know what I want. This is my desire. Give it to me." A woman can have so much more because she has a capacity, a specific definition, a knowledge of what she wants. But in that desire, she is not just say-ing, "Give it to me." To be sure, that exists (sometimes in great meas-ure), but it's not enough. Women also have a force within them that says, "You know what? I can't just sit still and RECEIVE. I feel like I have to do. I want to give. I want to earn what I have."

Women are so much more complicated than men. In fact, someone recently showed me a cartoon vividly illustrating that point. It was sim-ply a picture of a metal box. The top half said, "The Man." In the mid-dle of it was an on-off switch and a small light. That's all. The bottom half said, "The Woman." It was covered with any number of dials, knobs, switches, indicator lights, and gizmos large and small.

The Vessel, the female, is a creation that is a bit unbalanced. The woman has not just one aspect, receiving, but also sharing—two diver-gent aspects in the same person. If we want to understand why we may not feel equal to men, this is the reason. We are imbued with dual energy, and that is twice as much to handle.

It's in our nature to struggle with how much we can do. How often have I heard women complain, "What do they want from me? How much more can I shoulder? I work, take care of the kids, cook dinner, make birthday parties and Thanksgiving dinners, shop, and coach soc-cer, but I still need to find time for me—to have my nails done and my hair cut, to find a dress for my husband's fundraiser." Yes, yes, we undertake all of it, because it's in our nature as females to give as well as receive.

A man can say, "I go to work every day. That's what I know." But a woman must adapt to a multifaceted lifestyle. We have to juggle because we must create some kind of balance between sharing and receiving.

Interestingly, however, the discrimination against women that we may encounter in the spiritual world did not stem from a desire to deny women equal rights. The reason for it was exactly the opposite. Women did not need to pray as much as men because all of the energy of receiving and sharing is built in from the Endless World, from a time prior to the creation of men and women. Women are innately more spiritual beings. *The female is born with tremendous spiritual power, whereas the male has to earn his.*

So what looks to be the woman's dilemma is actually her advantage.

8

The Female Advantage

It is widely acknowledged that women are by nature more physically resilient than men—and anyone who has seen the movie *GI Jane* or has had a baby would not call that into question. In the uterus, the female fetus is stronger than that of the male. In fact, all embryos start off as female at the beginning of gestation, but at some point early in pregnancy, male hormones kick in and make a male out of the developing fetus. (On this level, all of us are truly receivers, except that we diverge into male and female manifestations of spiritual energy as time goes on.) There are more miscarriages of male fetuses than of female, and boys are less likely than girls to survive early childhood. Many diseases such as hemophilia pass through the mother to the male child but not to the female.

What is true physically is also true spiritually: Women are stronger; they have an innate knowledge. Research shows that women use more diverse regions of our brains and are capable of grasping nonverbal communication better than men. We've been given a gift of being more intuitive and, some might say, clairvoyant. We possess the ability to see things beyond our five senses into what kabbalists call the 99% world. A mother can sense that her child is sad, lonely, or hurting even if she's 1000 miles away.

These tools were given to us to nurture babies as well as to nourish the spiritual component between ourselves and our husbands. Indeed, we were created to be the spiritual leaders in the home. The woman is crown to the man. That's why she lights the candles on Friday night: It's her role to usher the Light into the house.

Many Hebrew expressions emphasize this important position: The woman of valor, the Shabbat queen, the Sabbath bride, the *shekinah* or feminine aspect of God. In fact, this is exactly why I decided to call this book *God Wears Lipstick*. We say that the woman builds and the woman destroys. By this we mean that what happens in her household is within her hands. The wife governs the amount of energy a home will have. She is the Light of that house. In fact, one of the things we learn in Kabbalah is that the moment a woman does not use her energy in order to build, she automatically destroys. There is no other option.

Why? Remember, women are subject to two forces operating at the same time: the sharing, caring, being able to juggle, giving, "cause" force, as well as that of being the "effect"—the wanting, taking, "me, me, me" victim energy. There is nothing in between.

Still, women are born to be helpmates. Females share naturally. Chimpanzees are the nearest living kin to our species, with a 99% overlap between their genes and our own. Those who study chimpanzees have found that the females of this species tend to rely on their female friends to insure their babies' survival. We are a nurturing, sharing, interdependent gender, especially when it comes to raising our babies—and we humans can point to play groups and babysitting co-ops to prove it.

People seem to feel that religion in general, and Judaism in particular, are chauvinistic, limiting the woman's role to raising children and taking care of the home—but this is actually not the case. In point of fact, *The Bible* is very clear about the spiritual importance of women.

9

Of Eve

A word here about *The Bible* must be added before we go on. Although the knowledge of how the universe functions is contained in the *Torah* (also known as the Five Books of Moses or the Old Testament), Rav Shimon bar Yochai explains that these stories are not meant to be understood merely on a literal level. Rather, they are intended as analogies or code for how the universe functions in a spiritual way. This encoding took place to teach us that in order for us to extract fulfillment, we must look deep inside. *The Zohar* deciphers the ancient scripture. In fact, it is a manual that explains, chapter by chapter, what each Bible story is really talking about.

Thus, *The Bible* is not just about religion or about what's allowed and prohibited. Rather, from the kabbalistic perspective, it's about the planets, it's about astrology, it's about the sun, it's about gravitation, it's about humankind, it's about reincarnation, it's about sharing, it's about love, and it's about the basic principles on which this universe is structured. So when I refer to *The Bible*, it's not from the point of view that this is information we should "believe in." Rather, this is truth that we *know with certainty*. What we have here is the manual to this universe.

That having been said, let's look at the first mention of the feminine in *The Bible*. Not surprisingly, it occurs with the creation of Eve. But Eve doesn't come along right away. On the sixth day of creation, God decided that he needed a Vessel into which he could pour his energy and his totality, so he created Adam. Adam was the first metaphor or person, and he was created to be the viaduct of all the energy that would ever be incurred in the world of Malchut, the world in which we live.

At the first instant of creation, Adam was given the totality of energy. So where was Eve? She hadn't been made yet. God decided that there needed to be a balance between positive energies. And toward that end, he created a division between the two levels of existence. Here is how it is written in *The Bible*: *"And God created man in His image, in the image of God He created Him; male and female He created them."*

In fact, each of us today is created male and female. In every male there's a bit of female (we talk about men getting "in touch with their feminine side") and in every female there's some male energy. This is even true hormonally. Men have estrogen circulating in their bodies and women testosterone, though in lesser amounts than in the opposite sex.

But this original male and female energy was still in potential form. If you read *The Bible* closely, you will find that Adam was not manifested until the second week, when the Creator breathed life into him and he became a living soul. Shortly after his creation, Adam was commanded to eat from every tree in the Garden of Eden except the Tree of Knowledge of good and evil. "As soon as you eat of it," God warned, "you shall die."

Then God became aware that Adam was lonely. "It's not good for man to be alone," He declared. After creating females of all the beasts and birds, God realized that Adam still didn't have an appropriate helpmate, so He put Adam into a deep sleep, and from one of his ribs the Creator *built* Eve.

I'd like to dwell for a moment on this word *built*. In fact, one of the ideas *The Zohar* teaches us is that none of the words in *The Bible* are there by coincidence; there's a reason each one is used. In Hebrew, the word *build* actually has three meanings. The first is knowledge or wisdom. *The Zohar* says that the woman received additional capacity for knowledge. This is not just about absorbing information but about transforming that information into practicality; it's about being able to process, to really learn and apply that knowledge to life. The second meaning is to understand. And the third refers to the power to build. These are among the attributes that the Creator gave to woman the moment he "built" Eve.

Since Eve was made *after* the Creator had admonished Adam to stay away from the Tree of Knowledge, she'd never heard the warning about the eating of its fruit. So why was she punished? She wasn't even on the scene yet. *The Zohar* explains that since Eve was inside

Adam—the female aspect was created on spiritual balance points— Eve could not be greater in her spiritual nature than Adam. She was his feminine spiritual counterpart, so instinctively she knew what she was and was not allowed to do. She understood the concept of negative influences, but she was tricked by the negative entity we've come to call the serpent. He tripped her, and she fell against the tree—and when she didn't die, he said to her, "You see. If you touched the Tree of Knowledge and didn't die, then God won't kill you. He only wants to deny you his knowledge. Go on. Taste the fruit."

Aren't we all familiar with this sort of behavior? We cheat a little bit and get away with it. So what happens? We cheat a little more and then a little more. We think we're never going to get caught, but eventually we become tangled in our own webs of deception.

Once Eve tasted the forbidden fruit, she offered it to her mate. Of course, Adam was punished as soon as he let on that he was aware of his nakedness. God cursed him and drove him from the Garden of Eden. According to *The Zohar*, God said to Adam, "Now you're going to be responsible for what happens to the next generation, and the next generation after that, and all generations throughout time, because you've forgotten that your channel of energy comes only from the Creator." Rather than receiving God's bounty and Light directly, man would now have to toil for his food by the sweat of his brow.

The time from Adam until the Great Flood is called the Age of Negativity. Evil took precedence because of mankind's inability to understand that men were only the channel of the Creator's energy. Therefore they misused their sexual functions in a way that created tremendous negativity in the world.

So what happened to Eve? She also fell. She was degraded, if you will, and forced to give birth in pain. She was made into a lesser entity. "Your urge shall be for your husband," said God, "and he shall rule over you." And thus women became chattel.

But as we'll see, they didn't remain so.

10

Sarah's Power

The situation remained pretty dismal for women until the time of Abraham the Patriarch. According to scripture, Abraham was the first person to believe in the one-God: Only one force reigned in this world, and everything fell under the canopy of this divine Creator. Abraham recognized that all the things that move the world come from that divine source and that he, as man, was a channel to bring the Light to the people.

Abraham underscored the fact that women were parallel and that their energy was equal to men's. He was the first leader to bring women to the forefront. Here's how it transpired:

Abram's wife Sarai was at an advanced age—well into menopause—and was unable to bear him any children. So she told her husband, in so many words, "Forget about me. You want a baby? Here's my Egyptian slave, Hagar. Make her your concubine and have a child with her. I'll raise the baby as my own." Abram followed his wife's directions, but as soon as Hagar became pregnant, she became disrespectful of her mistress, Sarai. This obviously presented problems. So Sarai complained to Abram.

His response? "The maid is in your hands. Deal with her as you think right."

Not surprisingly, Sarai was harsh with Hagar, who fled and took refuge in the desert. There she encountered the angel of God. He ordered her back to Sarai's tents with the promise that he would protect her offspring and increase them. She returned and eventually gave birth to Ishmael. Some years later, the angel of God came to Abraham (whose name had by then been altered to show that with his circumcision he had sealed his covenant with God) in the form of three male messengers. They promised that Sarah would have a son. Sarah laughed to herself, wondering, "Now that I am withered, am I to have enjoyment—with my husband so old?" Yet the Creator's power is mighty, and she did conceive and bear a child, Isaac.

Once again, dissension arose among Abraham's tents. As Sarah observed Isaac playing with Ishmael, she said to her husband, "Cast out the slave woman and her son." She didn't want Ishmael to share in her son's inheritance; the rivalry between the women was creating terrible chaos. This worried Abraham, so again he turned to the Creator.

The Creator's response? "Do not be troubled by this boy and your slave. *Whatever Sarah tells you, do as she says*, for it is through Isaac that offspring shall be continued to you."

So *The Zohar*, the knowledge of Kabbalah, tells us that according to cosmic law, a husband must listen to his wife. Whether or not we're aware of it, a woman is positioned such that if she decides that something should happen in a certain way, it will have to happen that way.

Many women experience this dynamic in their personal lives, but others don't recognize or own the power they have. This is often true of women in troubled marriages who come to me for counseling. Take Myra. "Whatever my husband says, goes," she complained, twisting a damp hankie in her shaking hands as she wept in my office. "Jonathan gets whatever he wants. So what am I doing wrong? Why does he chase other women? I give him everything he wants."

From *The Zohar*, we can see where the problem lies. Jonathan needs a challenge, not a doormat. He needs someone to stand up to him and say, "Hey, you're wrong."

In cases such as these, I ask the woman to look inside to see what makes her subservient. That attitude needs to be challenged. Myra, for instance, must recognize that she must become more assertive and lose the place of victim. Although she doesn't yet understand her responsibility in creating the negative environment (after all, from her point of view, Jonathan is cheating on *her*, and she gives in to his every whim), she has disconnected herself from her strength and lost herself.

Myra must ask, "What is the Light trying to teach me? I refuse to be led by my nose. I need to be an equal part of this relationship, not a subordinate." When she increases her self-esteem and understands that God's Light is as much a part of her as anyone else—that she has

Sarah's strength and power—she will start her journey toward transformation and the possible repair of her marriage.

The female spiritual advantage is real. Mothers have an inborn desire to share with their young and to maintain a home, whereas the male is by nature a wanderer. Women are more innately caring, loving, and nurturing. It is they who manifest love. Throughout history, whenever a problem needed solving through manifestation of the Light, it was a woman who brought resolution. In almost every great crisis, we know a woman was there to steer things right.

When the Israelites were about to be destroyed by the Egyptians, who threw every firstborn male into the sea, Batya, the daughter of the Pharaoh, took the little baby Moses from the water and reared him as her son in her own home. Indeed, the name *Moses* means "because I drew him out of the water." Had it not been for that assistance—the awakening of that energy in the world of Malchut—the man who would become the spiritual leader of Israel would have died in France, and there would never have been the seed by which the channel of the Light of the Creator would be revealed. This was manifested through the hand of Batya.

The greatest Light in history has always come through the hands of a woman. At Mount Sinai, when God gave *The Bible* to the people of Israel, He gave it first to the women. You probably also know the story of Esther, the heroine of the Purim saga, who saved her people from the evil of Haman in Persia.

Though we speak of our Bible as being chauvinistic, if we look at it carefully enough we will see that in every single instance where there was a lack of Light—where there was a darkness—a being or a metaphor that was a female entity representing the world of Malchut held on with her teeth and said, "I refuse to allow my spiritual energy to be diminished. I will not let that happen." At those times in our history, you will find revitalization and love born of the female capacity to mother a child. The metaphorical child needs the help, and the mother is there to softly and lovingly provide it.

The most spiritually influential moment occurred at the time of the Golden Calf.

11

A Turning Point:
The Golden Calf

Let's set the stage.

We're at Mount Sinai.

Here's the background.

Moses has taken the Israelites out of Egypt, from slavery into freedom, guided through the desert by the Creator's pillar of clouds by day and pillar of fire by night. He brings them to the Red Sea.

But Pharaoh has given chase, and the Israelites, trapped between the Red Sea and Pharaoh's fearsome army, lose faith. They are frightened. They demand of Moses, "Why did you bring us here? You took us into the wilderness to die." With the Creator's help, the sea splits in two, and the Israelites cross to the other side while Pharaoh's army is hurled into the waters. Miriam, the prophetess, sister of Moses and Aaron, picks up her timbrel and sings a song of praise on the far shore. Now Moses and the Israelites wander in the desert. The Creator provides them with *manna*. Moses leads them and deals with their grumblings and dissatisfactions—not enough water, boring food. They wander and wander, and finally they reach Mount Sinai. So what happens to Moses once they get there? He disappears. For 40 days he communes with God on Mount Sinai, receiving the Ten Commandments and the law. But the people don't know where he is. As far as they're concerned, he's gone.

So again there is grumbling, restlessness, rebellion in the air. "We have no idea what happened to Moses," they say. "Maybe he's not coming back at all. Maybe he ran away."

So the men gather around Aaron, and they demand, "Make us an oracle, a god, to lead us." At that time in history, idol worship was still prevalent. So in Moses' absence, the nation of Israel demanded of his brother that he create some kind of statue for them to pray to. They had lost certainty in the Creator.

Aaron complies. He tells the men, "Take off the gold rings that are on the ears of your wives, your sons and daughters." These are to be melted down to form the Golden Calf.

This is the pivotal moment.

Notice that Aaron sent the men to their wives to take from them their gold. Why did he have to send them? Why didn't the women offer up the precious metal willingly?

The Zohar explains to us that at this point the women refused to participate. "What's the rush?" they asked. "Moses will come back. Have certainty." The women didn't even gather around Aaron. So the men went to their wives and ripped the gold from their bodies to build the calf.

The sages of Kabbalah tell us that the women were unwilling participants. They would not allow themselves to be a Vessel for anything less than the Light of the Creator; they did not accept the Golden Calf and the idea of idolatry. Until this crucial moment, when women understood and chose to use their power, Eve's curse was still upon them, and men still treated them like chattel. Not until they saw that the Golden Calf would cause a break in the spiritual system—and that the men had lost sight of the purpose for which they were created—could the women themselves become elevated.

Now the consequences.

Kabbalah explains to us that at this moment, women finished their correction. Their job was done. What Eve couldn't fix in the Garden of Eden was now set right. No longer was it a question of "Me, me, me. What's going to happen to me?" They made more dominant the Light, certainty, and restriction.

However, Kabbalah also says that since women are now corrected, *the only people who still need correcting are men.* They were unable to practice or exercise the desire to restrict. They did not have certainty.

Therefore, men must go through many more stages and tests in the growth process than do women.

What does this mean to us today?

Women are born with tremendous spiritual power, whereas men must earn theirs. Indeed, *The Zohar* teaches us that the least spiritual woman on earth still has the potential to be the greatest psychic, which means she has the ability to see beyond the limitations of her senses. God, indeed, does wear lipstick.

And what does it mean to be spiritual? We may think it has to do with reading certain books, practicing yoga, meditating, or learning about astrology. But Kabbalah explains to us that spirituality is about accepting that our whole reason for being is to share. It awakens us to an understanding that we need to improve ourselves. Spirituality is about being able to see what's wrong with ourselves, accepting the idea that we can change, and then showing a willingness to actually transform ourselves. Rather than relying on an ego that says, "I'm okay and the rest of the world is a problem," it's the capacity to say, "I'm willing to see that I need to improve myself, and I'm willing to give before I take."

Within women's DNA there continues to be this force or energy from the time of the Golden Calf—an understanding of the power of conti-nuity, the power of restriction, the power of sharing. And at that point it was also determined that unless we are attuned to the energy of spirituality, we will always feel foreign in this world. The moment we turn to spirituality, it awakens us.

This is the reason, at least in the Jewish world, that women are not required to pray. It's not because they are discriminated against, but because they don't need to. Even though it may be hard for us to remember those pivotal moments at Mount Sinai, we should proceed with the knowledge that we have already been corrected and are automatically more spiritual than men, for whom correction is a far more arduous task.

12

So Why Are We Here?

At this point you may be scratching your head and asking, "Hey, just a minute. If we women are corrected, and if it was all taken care of at the time of the Golden Calf—if we already have certainty; if we understand the harmony between the plus and the minus, between the sharing and giving, between having a desire and restriction (your basic delayed gratification); if we've already learned to share in order to receive—*why are we here?*

The answer to this perplexing question is simple: Women are endowed with a special responsibility. We are here to help our men with their correction and to help manifest Light in the world.

But before we examine this concept more closely, I want you to understand that it doesn't mean we're superior to men. There is no "higher" or "lower" order to human beings. Men and women have different but inseparable functions. To use the metaphor of the light bulb once again, the light glows because there is harmony between the negative and positive charges. It is an integrated system—one in which one part cannot function without the other.

That having been said, however, how often have we heard our friends (or ourselves) complain about a male partner, "What a baby. He behaves like a child." Why do we use such language to describe our adult relationships?

What we usually mean is that men are innocent and naïve in an important way; they lack certain tools of metaphysical understanding. So we say, "They don't get it." Why? Because from the time of the Golden Calf, men are not corrected. They don't have spiritual knowledge from within the way women do. It's not in their nature.

We may think this places men at a disadvantage, but there are many positive aspects to such naïveté. Men often don't carry around the burden and the responsibility of that need to give as well as to receive—all that complicated stuff that we women cope with. For them, life is simpler. But it's up to us women to shape their energy so that they learn to use the good and eliminate the bad, just as we do with our young children.

FINDING TRUE HAPPINESS

You may look to the time of the Golden Calf and wonder, what's the connection to my life today? After all, that was during biblical times, but I'm here now, in the 21st century.

When we deal with spirituality, we must remember that time, space, and motion have no influence in the spiritual world. And 99% of our being is spiritual. You can't define the feeling of fulfillment or happiness. Is it a cup? Is it a bucket? Can you measure how long or wide or tall your happiness is? All the desires we have in life—happiness, love, security, support—are completely metaphysical, which is to say that they are without physical substance. There may be physical applications to these desires, but in essence they are totally spiritual.

This is also true of cosmic law. Although we personally weren't at Mount Sinai and did not ourselves reject the building of the Golden Calf the way the Israelite women did, from that time forward our role in the universe did not change. According to Kabbalah, whatever else has taken place in history matters little. The spiritual role of women— *why we are here*—is to assist the male aspect in correcting itself. And in that, we are to find true happiness.

So how does this emerge in our daily lives? From a very early age, most girls are in a rush to get married. We often feel empty as single women, as if something were missing, and yearn not just for a man but the right man. It's as if we're saying, "Let's get the job done. I came here for a purpose. Where are you already?"

Yet the moment we find the man and get hitched, we say, "Next." And off we go to the next stage in our lives.

The reason women feel this urge, which men don't experience until much later in their lives, doesn't stem from some psychological, sociological, or biological ticking clock. Rather, it springs from an aspect of our soul. We were put on earth with a sense of purpose.

Men do not have the same consciousness. In fact, men married in the Jewish world wear *talit* that are placed on their foreheads at the time of their wedding. A certain piece of silver rests there too, but most men don't realize what this is. They like the silver plaque because they perceive it as prestigious. But Kabbalah teaches us that this piece of silver says, "The moment I get married, I accept upon myself the desire to change and improve myself." It's not about prestige. Rather, it allows a consciousness that says the man is operating as one with his wife. Just as with Adam and Eve, "A man leaves his father and mother and clings to his wife, so they may become one flesh."

And her role? To improve him, to correct him, to give shape to his energy, to assist in his correction.

13

Our Other Half

Why must we women correct our male aspect? Let's go back to that seminal moment in *The Bible* that describes God creating Adam. Here it is again: *"And God created man in His image, in the image of God He created Him; male and female He created them."*

Kabbalah explains that every soul is combined from a female aspect and a male aspect. Each soul has two halves: male and female. This means that each and every one of us has another half, a male counterpart in this world—the other half of our soul. It's what we've come to call our *soulmate*.

This also means that the feminine aspect of our soul, although corrected, will never be completed until our male aspect is corrected as well. How can this be accomplished? Sometimes it takes many lifetimes. Indeed, like many Eastern spiritual traditions, Kabbalah teaches that our souls reincarnate time and time again until the job is done.

REINCARNATION

We come down to this world when we're born, do whatever work we must, make some corrections, and perhaps mess up in other ways, and then we die. At that moment, our souls leave the body and elevate to a place in which their physical confines no longer exist. Actually, we die for one of two reasons. On the one hand, we've achieved what we were supposed to accomplish spiritually in this lifetime, and we're clear, clean, and corrected. There's no purpose in our soul being here anymore, so back it goes to reside eternally in the Light of the Creator. Or, on the other hand, we die because there's no way we're going to achieve the correction in this lifetime. When the body cannot serve the purpose of the soul to improve, change, and elevate itself, we need a new body.

Then, when we're ready, we incarnate once more and are given a new stage that allows for the continued process of correction. Maybe that new body must be born in Afghanistan and not in New York City or Los Angeles. Maybe this time we'll be brilliant scientists and not starving artists. In fact, we are reborn in this way, time and again, until our souls achieve a purified form.

Kabbalah also teaches, however, that a female soul cannot be forced to incarnate and come down to this world. It's a choice she makes. Even God Himself cannot force a woman to incarnate because she doesn't have to, as women are already corrected from the time of the Golden Calf. That means a woman doesn't have her own karma, or a sense of purpose, with which to work out negative aspects of her own self— such as hate for no reason, jealousy, arrogance, or rage. So there's a different reason for female souls to come back to earth. It's not as if we're bored up there, and there's nothing else to do. We chose to come down.

But why?

A female chooses to incarnate—to come back to this world of *Malchut*—in order to assist the male aspect of her soul in correcting himself.

So you may look at your husband, scratch your head, and ask in disbelief, "I volunteered for him? How can this be?" We often feel this way because we live in a fragmented world and are not easily connected with our sense of spirituality. But our souls can still sense or feel our purpose and the original reason for the attraction.

Or perhaps you might ask, "How can this be? We don't always meet our male counterparts in this lifetime. Some women never marry; they may not even want to. Others choose to share their lives with another woman. Where is the male aspect of *their* souls?"

But we're talking about the cosmos here—the bigger picture. When we look at the reasons underlying how this universe operates, it becomes clear that every soul has two aspects: male and female. The Torah says that the female must sometimes wait a long time before her male soulmate creates a spiritual environment that's right for her. The two parts of the soul do not necessarily come down to this planet at the same time, which is why there can be great age differences when they do reunite. Sometimes a woman is even put into a relationship with someone else until her soulmate is ready for her. We see this in the instance of David and Batsheba. Uriah, Batsheba's first husband, was given to Batsheba until the time came for her to join David.

In fact, it's not always necessary for a woman to marry her true soulmate. Sometimes she has to marry him in order to get the job done, and sometimes she doesn't. If the souls are deemed lucky enough or have worked hard enough on their spiritual goals, they are allowed to marry. That is a soulmate union—one in which the two souls have been part of each other for all eternity.

PART II

KABBALISTIC

TOOLS

First, a Word About . . .

I have just finished sharing with you the wisdom of *The Zohar* as it applies to women. As you've been reading, you might have thought, as would be typical of most women, "This is interesting. Insightful, really. I can see where it makes sense. But what do I do with it? How do I put it to use in my own life?"

That's what Part II is all about.

What follows is a series of kabbalistic tools that will help you on your spiritual journey of transformation.

Underlying many of these tools is the theme of developing and maintaining meaningful relationships. I've done this on purpose. Why?

1

The Number One Kabbalistic Tool Is Relationships.

If our relationships serve us in the way

the Light intended, they become

wonderful opportunities for

spiritual growth and transformation.

According to Kabbalah, whether or not you see its significance at the time, everything in your life happens for a reason. Although you might believe this statement intellectually, if you look honestly at your life, you'll probably find that you don't act as though a beautiful design were really behind each event. Most people think their experiences are mostly random coincidences. According to Kabbalah, however, there is no such thing as a coincidence. Everything is preordained.

That being true, any challenge you encounter in life is part of a design *whose intent is to help you grow and change.* The more arduous the difficulty, the greater the opportunity it affords you to mend your ways in order to connect to the Light. This is true even of the worst situations. In fact, the more negativity there is in an interaction, the more potential there will be to reveal Light.

So in your daily comings and goings, which experiences provide the greatest potential for you to make this transformation toward the Light? Which offer the most opportunities for giving and sharing? Those that occur within your relationships, of course.

Look at your life, and you will see that most of the challenges you face stem from your interactions with others. Your life is all about relationships—with your parents, siblings, lovers, spouses, children, grandchildren, aunts and uncles, cousins, friends, neighbors, colleagues, bosses, employees, the mailman, the nanny, your doctor, your gardener . . . You name it—if it's part of your life, it has a relationship attached to it.

In this book, however, we'll be focusing on intimate partnerships—husbands or partners—because as we have seen, these important men in our lives constitute our other half, the Light to our Vessel, for whose purpose we have decided to take the plunge and reincarnate.

Suppose, for instance, you keep finding yourself in the same relationship drama—you're continually attracted to unavailable (or married) men, or the men whom you're with tend to be overbearing and domineering. The reason is simple: *You have not yet learned a certain lesson that life is presenting to you.* When you view relationships from this kabbalistic perspective, you will have a different experience of them, and you will be able to make the changes that are necessary for your transformation.

Understanding this is the key tool to developing a positive attitude, because it means you can stop blaming other people for what goes wrong—that is, you can stop being an effect and become a cause.

I once counseled a couple, Mike and Rosemary, who obviously loved each other but had difficulty making a commitment. They were both fiercely independent. I could tell they were afraid of losing what they would call their "freedom." Mike blamed Rosemary and Rosemary blamed Mike, but they were equally reluctant to throw themselves head over heels into love.

This was not the first time the commitment issue had been a problem for them. Before they'd met, they had both been involved with others who were somewhat guarded and emotionally unavailable. "In this city, women tend to be cool and independent," Mike told me, implying that the problem lay not with him but with the women he dated. On another occasion, Rosemary had made a similar comment about the men she had known.

Of course, the pool of potential partners from which we draw is never the issue. On the contrary. We are attracted to those who reveal unresolved issues in our own lives—the *tikune* we have come to earth to correct. Those whom we draw to us usually resonate on the same frequency as we do and are therefore just like us, even if they may appear to be different on the surface.

I explained this to Mike and Rosemary and told them that they were really in the same boat. Neither of them truly wanted to make a commitment because doing so would mean addressing fears that they were hiding not only from each other but from themselves. They were not yet ready to take real responsibility for themselves and become proactive, to make no mention of taking responsibility for all the issues that come up in a committed relationship. Both unconsciously needed to meet emotionally unavailable people so that they wouldn't run the risk of exposing their fears or of having to do the tremendous work that arises when you allow yourself to become deeply intimate with another person.

As I worked with Mike and Rosemary, it became clear to me that they both had difficulty trusting others, trusting themselves, and ultimately trusting the Light. This was the root of their problems, and it was the reason they kept attracting partners who brought this basic lack of trust to the surface.

Once Rosemary and Mike became aware of the deeper layers of their situation and their own patterns, they began to open up to each other in ways that had never been possible before. They stopped trying to change each other and instead began to understand their own commitment fears. Although their relationship ended a year later, it still did its job by helping this couple grow. Even though they did not clear up all their trust issues once and for all (this can be a lifelong task for some), both enjoyed a period of intimacy that neither had ever experienced in previous relationships. The breakup occurred without resentment because Mike and Rosemary finally understood and respected each other. Neither felt victimized; both simply realized that they were better as friends than as lovers, so they made a mutual, proactive decision to end their romantic involvement.

Recently, Rosemary met someone who is an exceptionally open and warm—hearted person with a generous nature. Evidently, Rosemary is no longer stuck in her old pattern of attracting emotionally distant men. She learned what she needed to learn from her struggles with Mike and was able to elevate herself as a result. She would never have connected with a man like this in the past, but once she was ready, he appeared.

If you have not yet come across your lifelong partner, I believe that you, too, can find that person, provided you do the necessary work on yourself. This may involve:

- learning to make choices in your life that have the effect of clearing rather than clouding your vision

- learning to become proactive instead of reactive

- learning to be a sharer rather than a receiver-for-the-self-alone

- learning to practice restriction

Indeed, in the pages that lie ahead, I will introduce you to many beautiful ways of connecting with and using the wisdom of Kabbalah, especially when it comes to obtaining dramatic improvements in your relationships.

Kabbalah teaches us that we are on a spiritual journey. It teaches that life has a marvelous objective that we are ultimately assured of reaching. The purpose of our relationships is to help us get to our destination. When we learn to look at our relationships in this way, we become aware of the beautiful gifts they contain, and we begin to travel more quickly along our path.

If our relationships serve us in the way the Light intended, they become wonderful opportunities for spiritual growth and transformation.

2

Reclaim Your Power:
The Sharing Tool

*You should ask yourself,
"On my journey through life,
how much good have I done?"*

Marion Preminger was born in a fairy-tale castle in Hungary and was raised like a princess. She met Otto Preminger in Vienna. They married and moved to Los Angeles, where Otto's career as a movie director took off. He soon became rich and famous, and they became one of Hollywood's most admired couples. But the stress of life in the fast lane took its toll on Marion. She battled addictions to alcohol and drugs and became notorious for her affairs.

When Otto finally divorced Marion, her life collapsed completely. She made three unsuccessful suicide attempts. Finally, she left California and returned to Vienna. There she met Albert Schweitzer, the legendary medical doctor, musician, philosopher, theologian, and missionary. He was home on leave from his hospital in Africa.

Schweitzer fascinated Marion. During the remainder of his European visit, she spent every day with him. When it came time for Schweitzer to return to Africa, she begged him to allow her to accompany him, and he agreed. She spent the rest of her life in the Lambarene Hospital in Gabon, emptying bedpans, changing bandages, and bathing lepers.

In her autobiography, *All I Want is Everything*, Marion wrote: "Albert Schweitzer says there are two kinds of people. There are the helpers, and the non-helpers. I thank God He allowed me to become a helper, and in helping, I found everything."

* * *

If you spend most of your life chasing after something that doesn't respond to your deepest desire for fulfillment, you will ultimately feel empty and joyless. You consist of both body and soul. Thus, if you work only to satisfy your physical desires—your body—and ignore the yearnings of your soul, you will starve this all-important aspect of your being.

Everything material fades, so there is no way it can give lasting satisfaction. To be sure, it is wonderful to live in a beautiful home and have many lovely jewels and fancy cars. I am not suggesting that you should not want these things or that you should follow Marion Preminger's example and make a pilgrimage to Africa. I am simply saying that you should ask yourself, *"On my journey through life, how much good have I done?"* Remember, Kabbalah teaches that women are complex creatures: We are by nature both receivers and sharers.

There is a Jewish law forbidding the destruction of a fruit-bearing tree growing on your property. This is in reality a lovely spiritual instruction about how you should live your life. You may be beautiful, in your hands may be great tools, and millions of people may love you—but if you have not given yourself over to the creation of something special for someone else, then everything you have received will be for naught. This is what the fruit-bearing tree symbolizes: You must share of yourself in a way that permanently improves the quality of life in this world. Ultimate, deep, lasting fulfillment can come only when your soul is fed, and the only food that satisfies the soul is what comes from unconditional sharing.

It is said that the Desire to Receive for the Self Alone is the root of all evil. The original Vessel in the Endless World experienced Bread of Shame with great discomfort, and it is one of the basic teachings of Kabbalah that applies equally to your life as an individual and to your relationships. Spending too much time concentrating on yourself—the gravitational pull of "me, me, me"—is the seed of all problems. If your thoughts and actions focus only on your needs—on what you can get out of a situation—then you are operating from a perspective of lack. It is clear that this can never lead to happiness and fulfillment. Remember, when you worry only about yourself, the Creator can't come in. There is no room, because someone is already there looking after you.

A sense of entitlement and the act of complaining are two clear-cut indicators that you're mired in Bread of Shame. You're the effect; you're sitting back waiting for someone to give to you. You think they owe you. You've made someone else the source of your happiness, and when he doesn't live up to your expectations or needs, you whine, grumble, and maybe even nag. In truth, however, only you can be the source of your own happiness.

Besides, only when you worry about others—when you become genuinely concerned with their needs—does the Creator see *your* needs. Your preoccupation with others will crowd out the time you spend on anxious self-concern. By transforming the Desire to Receive for the Self Alone into a Desire to Receive for the Sake of Sharing, you will connect with the Creator, and your experience of life will be transformed.

Kabbalah teaches that you are given a choice: Either you can use the extraordinarily powerful force of desire in a destructive way, or you can turn it around and use it so that it can become pure Light.

Remember the metaphor of the light bulb? You generate Light when you "restrict," or hold back, your habitual negative, selfish reactions and allow your proactive, sharing nature to emerge. This doesn't imply that you must repress your feelings. It's just a question of becoming conscious so that you can loosen their hold on you a little, thereby allowing that other part of you—the sharing nature of the Light—to be revealed in all its luminescence and glory.

If you and your partner enjoy a higher purpose of sharing with the world—if you put your energy into something worthwhile outside yourselves—then your relationship will blossom. When you connect with the Light, you bring true joy and vitality into your life. This is the beautiful result of unconditional sharing, because it transforms your essence into that of the Creator. When you share, you create a circuit through which all the gifts you have been given, including the gift of your relationship, flow in a continuous cycle. Your life then becomes truly rich, and you are filled with appreciation for everything you have.

If, on the other hand, you receive without sharing, the result is stagnation. Just as trapped water becomes putrid, so does Light energy become stagnant when its flow is blocked. There is nothing wrong with receiving; you're supposed to receive—but if there is no sharing, then what you receive is limited and unfulfilling.

When you share, you create a circuit of loving energy, and the Light of the Creator, which then comes into your life, protects the two of you— giving you a level of contentment and fulfillment that you can never receive if you try to grab happiness in a self-centered way. If you base your relationship on unconditional sharing, a bond is created between you and your partner that is the greatest of all gifts.

3

Slip into Something Uncomfortable: The Effort Tool

Ultimately,

it is your greatest challenges

that bring the greatest gifts.

Of course, no one said this would be easy. In fact, many Kabbalah students ask why it takes so much work to make progress in life, particularly in relationships. Why is it so difficult?

The reason often surprises them.

In reality, we wouldn't have it any other way. Something in human nature—an aversion to Bread of Shame—makes us want to earn what we receive. We enjoy a challenge. Would golf be enjoyable if you got a hole in one every time you hit the ball? Where's the fun in that? You'd soon lose interest in the game.

I often like to tell a story about Bonnie of the infamous couple-on-a-crime-spree, Bonnie and Clyde. In this story, Bonnie gets killed in that famous Depression-era shootout. She then goes to heaven and meets a greeter at the door—let's says he's an angel. He's dedicated to her and has been placed there to provide for all of her needs.

"What would you like?" he asks kindly.

"I'd like to go to the south of France on a private yacht," Bonnie replies. "And I'd like to have people serving me."

"Done." says the angel.

In a blink, Bonnie is cruising the Mediterranean with servants gathered all around her, tending to her every whim. But by the end of the first week on the Riviera, she's bored silly. She calls for her angel. "I've had enough of this," she complains. "I need to do something exciting. In fact, I'd prefer to rob banks."

"Okay," he responds gamely. "Which bank? What town? At what time?" They sit down and plan the heist.

Bonnie comes to the town at the appointed hour. What a shock. The bank's doors are standing wide open. In fact, the vault is yawning at her, ready to disgorge its riches. The tellers hand her the money with a smile. There's not even a guard on duty to stop her. She can stroll out of there without messing a single hair on her head. There's no anxiety, no worry.

Bonnie becomes furious. "Wait a minute," she demands of her angel. "Where's the chase? Where are the cops? This is too easy. Where's the challenge?"

"Sorry," he says, "but there is no challenge here."

"Well, then, I hate this place." Bonnie exclaims. "There's no action. Nothing to make me satisfied. I don't want to stay in Heaven. Send me to Hell," she demands.

"And where do you think you are?" the angel asks.

* * *

In relating this story, I am by no means condoning bank robbery, of course. But my point is that while you may complain about your struggle, when you truly understand the process you're in, you'll realize that everything is as it needs to be—and that you wouldn't have it any other way.

Effort is an expression of a deep desire in the soul. It takes hard work to get emotional and spiritual growth right. So take heart if your relationship is a struggle. With consciousness and persistence, you can change the way you relate to your partner, and you will enjoy your improved relationship all the more for having worked hard on it.

Ultimately, it is your greatest challenges that bring the greatest gifts. If you're struggling in your relationship, remember that you are being offered a great chance for happiness. But if you approach your difficulties from the perspective of a victim—if you fall into reactivity, entitlement, or a cry of "me, me, me"—then you will experience little if any growth.

Look inside; be honest with yourself. Are you actually creating your difficulties? By working on yourself and transforming that flawed, negative aspect of your character—which is what drew the situation to you in the first place—you remove the need to experience the situation in the future.

To become a truly fulfilled person, be prepared to undergo every kind of trial. Without the pressure, the fight, the work, it is impossible to transform yourself. Without the struggle, there is no reward. We're all like lumps of coal: If you simply dig the coal from the ground, its nature doesn't change. You must apply thousands of pounds of pressure to transform it into a diamond.

The work of evolving spiritually is inherently difficult. We strive to grow, and each time we fall down, we pick ourselves up and carry on. We are in a constant battle with the negative part of ourselves. But each time we resist the negativity, we reconnect to the Light and are rewarded in return with the ability to shine.

4

How to Read the Signs:
The Astrology Tool

The key is to remember that

there is always a lot more going on

in a person than

what appears on the surface.

To understand someone's sign is to understand their nature.

Kabbalah has been using astrology as a tool for 4000 years. In the *Sefer Yetzirah*, or *The Book of Formation*, written by Abraham the Patriarch, it is said that the planets of our solar system are devices that imprint an individual's spiritual nature on the soul. Your soul was responsible for determining the most propitious moment of birth. It chose the specific arrangement of planets that would influence its incarnation.

How does this help with your relationships? It's simple. If you know that planetary configurations influence your partner's temperament, you will be less tempted to blame him. Does this mean that he's not responsible for his own behavior? Of course not. It just means that his personality style expresses the "hand he was dealt." The good news is that with knowledge of his sign, you can work with his personality rather than against it. Life flows a lot more easily when it's lived in harmony with astrological temperament.

When the Rav and I were first married, many aspects of our relationship were challenging. However, they became easier to handle once I understood how his astrological sign influenced his character.

My husband is a Leo, a sign that needs loads of attention and care. If you want something from a Leo, you compliment him and tell him how great he is. This may seem like flattery or manipulation, but it's not. Rather, it's a way of circumventing the negative and bringing out your partner's positive aspects.

Leo is one of the fire signs, which are known to anger easily. (The other two fire signs are Aries and Sagittarius.) Leos also tend to have problems of ego. Therefore, it is unwise to confront a Leo partner's ego by saying, for example, "When you were talking to that couple, you didn't always hear the woman's point of view." It's better if you first emphasize strengths: "It was wonderful how you helped that couple with their problem." Allow your Leo to bask in his glory, and then, while he is basking, you can add, "Oh, and by the way, there was this one thing you could have handled a little bit differently."

If your partner is an air sign (Gemini, Libra, or Aquarius), he is capable of accomplishing many tasks at once. Air signs are active and easily become impatient. Used to getting things done quickly, they are always onto the next thing even before they've signed the last deal. If you live with one, you know what I am talking about. You must allow this part of your partner's nature to bloom, or you will have a depressed man on your hands.

Earth signs (Taurus, Virgo, and Capricorn) can have particular difficulty with air signs. Their nature is usually slower, which causes a clash of styles that can easily lead to conflict. But it doesn't have to be this way. Again, tolerance is the key. By recognizing that we all have different natures, the earth sign can develop an accepting attitude toward her air-sign partner. Simply appreciate his ability to speed through tasks, and give him the freedom to do the projects that he loves and needs to do. If he streaks ahead, don't hold him back. The earth sign can catch up in her own good time, knowing that she has her own strong points, which are different and complementary.

When your air-sign partner has finished his frenetic activities, leave him the luxury of lounging on the couch and doing nothing. This is the way he becomes more creative. Don't pull on his kite strings. If you allow him to soar, it will make a wonderful difference in your relationship.

Some signs are typically more sensitive than others, especially the water signs (Cancer, Scorpio, and Pisces). Cancers are quick to feel insulted, so the worst thing you can do to a Cancer is criticize him directly. Don't say, "You were being inconsiderate when you . . . " Instead, solicit his empathy: "Can you imagine how I might feel when you do that?" Or "Do you know how much I love you and how much it bothers me when this sort of thing happens?" You will evoke a completely different response from a Cancer if you approach him from a stance of compassion rather than confrontation. This sign cannot deny the "how you made me feel" perspective because it resonates with Cancer's own emotional makeup. Matching your partner's style in this way is a simple technique that can improve your relationship overnight.

Being an emotional sign, Cancers have many ups and downs. Never argue with a Cancer when he's angry or depressed; it simply doesn't work. The best you can do is walk away, give him space, let him figure it out, and wait for him to come back. Then perhaps you will have a chance to straighten things out with him. If you approach an issue with criticism or impatience, you will end up with a hostile partner on your hands.

These examples demonstrate the benefits of knowing your partner's astrological traits. It is also helpful to know your own sign and its strengths and weaknesses. If you are to reconnect with the Light, you must stop your reactive nature as it arises. Astrology helps you become aware of your reactive tendencies, which makes it easier for you to work with them. Moreover, when you know your own frailties more intimately, you become more compassionate toward yourself— which is an important part of developing patience and love for others. I can give only a brief introduction to astrology here, but there are many resources you can use if you wish to learn more. I suggest that you pay special attention to books focusing on spiritual astrology, since these will give you tools with which to understand your own and your partner's spiritual makeup.

You may not become an expert astrologer, but that's not the goal here. In the end, even if you don't understand exactly what your partner is experiencing, you'll appreciate that there is a lot more going on within him than what appears on the surface. It takes work to understand a person deeply, but there are great rewards awaiting you if you are willing to become a compassionate and understanding person. As I've explained, life rarely hands relationship success to us on a plate. Effort is required.

5

Hurry Up and Be Patient:
The Tolerance Tool

*There is so much good
in the worst of us and
so much bad in the best of us
that it ill behooves any of us
to find fault with others.*

One of the key ingredients to developing a loving relationship is tolerance. Intolerance is the opposite of love, since it is judgmental and rejecting, which love is not. Tolerance gives us the flexibility we need to grow. A reed will bend in the wind, but a mighty tree can crack and topple in that same gust because it is so inflexible. As your tolerance and understanding grow, you will discover that more love will enter your relationships. These are aspects of the Creator, and as you begin to practice tolerance, the Light will glow in your life.

Tolerance is central to the teachings of Kabbalah because it yields human dignity. Yet it requires constant practice. Allow others to be themselves in all your relationships. Focus on yourself and take responsibility for what's happening with you—after all, you've attracted this man to you—but don't try to "fix" your partner. Take him as he is. Tolerance means seeing the negative aspects of your partner's personality and being able to accept him, flaws and all, just as you would expect him to accept you. This is the highest form of respect, and it is true unconditional love.

Tolerance does not mean, however, that you should stand by while your husband is messing around with other women or behaving arrogantly toward you. I'm not asking you to tolerate his bad behavior. Remember that Sarah's power is part of your spiritual DNA.

The concept of tolerance may cause some confusion, especially since I've explained that a woman's role is to participate in her husband's "correction." The idea here is that you must recognize why your partner behaves as he does in your relationship. When you identify what this brings up *for you* and start working on it *in you*, you'll be well on your way toward making that correction. Help your partner solve the issues for himself—not because they're part of your agenda but because they're part of his. When you're nonjudgmental rather than berating ("As for me, it's okay if you stay the way you are"), then he'll be much more likely to hear you and work on himself, for himself.

The Light of the Creator manifests in the world in a particular way for each person. Everyone has a specific job to do, and we're each a perfect aspect of God's plan. If your mate is a difficult person—perhaps he acts like a boor or is egocentric or lazy—you might gnash your teeth and think, "I can't cope with him." If you had been given his process of correction (his *tikune*), however, you'd be exactly like him.

Understanding that people are sent into the world with different tasks that are as specific to them as their fingerprints will help you become naturally more tolerant. If the Creator made someone a certain way, He did so in order to give that person an opportunity to change.

He did the same for you. He gave you specific challenges to work with so that you could transform your nature.

If you find it difficult to tolerate someone—if you're really furious with him—think of three things you love about him. Ask yourself, is this behavior worth destroying the relationship over? And remember that you are no different than he. You also have much to correct. Souls reincarnate together; this is a path your soul has chosen. Therefore, it's wise to be compassionate and accepting. After all, there is so much good in the worst of us and so much bad in the best of us, it ill behooves any of us to find fault with others.

6

Do You Want to Know a Secret?
The Listening Tool

You may hear

what your partner says,

but this isn't always

true listening.

The best way to develop tolerance in your life is to learn the art of compassionate listening. It is a basic human need to be able to share one's innermost thoughts and feelings without fear of judgment. You don't have to agree with everything your partner or friends tell you, but if you are nevertheless willing to listen, you give them a beautiful gift. Listening means stepping outside of yourself. It's the most powerful part of sharing.

In today's world, listening is a lost art. You may hear what your partner says, but like being aware of the background noise of a blaring radio or television, this isn't always true listening. Hearing and listening are not synonymous.

If you want to become a person with whom others feel safe to express themselves, start each day by setting the intention to listen. When you wake up, you could say a prayer that asks for support. Here's one: *"Open my ears to the universe, and let me be cognizant of all that's around me. Let me feel the vibration of those whom I love, so that I am attuned to them. Let me be surrounded by positive energy and fully receptive to everyone around me."*

By the way, prayer and meditation are the way to dial into consciousness. Spiritual events occur almost exactly the same way physical events do. The only difference is that you are usually unaware of the spiritual connections you make. On a physical level, when you dial a telephone, you expect to get a response on the other end. On the spiritual level, the same thing happens: When you pray, you are dialing the higher dimension. You may not hear the receiver being picked up at the other end, but when you reach out to the Creator in this way, you are heard.

You can ask for help in empathic listening at any time:

- When you talk with your mate during the day, you can ask for the energy to help you be completely in his shoes, and it will come to you.

- Pray that you not feel or hear anything other than him and imagine that you are setting yourself aside.

- When your partner speaks, ask to be able to feel his spirit, his energy, and to relate to him on his level, whatever that might be.

There is no such thing as "higher" or "lower." Use your tolerance tool: Don't judge where your partner is in his life; just try to relate to him in a way that his eyes, ears, and mind will understand.

If you practice these tools and techniques on a regular basis, they will become easier. Whenever you make a sincere effort to be more conscious, positive energy—the Light—will always come in to assist you.

7

Never Be a Victim:
The Interdependence Tool

An interdependent relationship requires two people who are spiritually mature enough to stand on their own two feet.
The first question you should ask yourself is, "Do I have that level of maturity myself?"

We hear a lot about codependent relationships nowadays. You know you're in a one when there's lots of manipulation going on between you and your partner.

When this is the situation, you may profess to love each other, but in fact there will be little genuine love. Rather, the relationship comes down to a series of destructive power struggles. You try to control each other because you are desperate to get your own needs met. You're both mired in Bread of Shame, each wanting to receive for the self alone.

Sadly, you'll never be fulfilled in this way. Fulfillment doesn't emanate from feeding selfish desires. Fulfillment doesn't come from feeling entitled or dependent. Fulfillment doesn't emerge from being an effect, a victim. Where does it come from? Unconditional sharing. That means reversing the flow of energy from taking to giving. When you do this, you bring the Light into the relationship, and the Light takes care of you.

In a healthy relationship, you and your partner are interdependent. You are like the sun and the moon. The moon doesn't need the sun to rise, and the sun doesn't need the moon to set. But they do need each other to activate the universe.

You'll have a better relationship if you're separate and self-sufficient in this regard—if you are your own Light. You each have your own nature, but you will find that your journey through life is more beautiful and offers many more opportunities for spiritual growth when you take it together.

Enjoying spending time with your partner is natural. You should want that. However, a healthy togetherness is not based on a sense of inadequacy or neediness. Each of you strives individually to become a more loving, Light-filled human being. At the same time, you have a love for each other and a compatibility in ideas and values that glue you together as a couple.

But this doesn't mean you agree about everything. In fact, sometimes saying "no"—performing seemingly unsharing acts—can be just what your partner needs. So can walking away. Sometimes you just won't see eye to eye on important issues.

I can tell you this from personal experience. The Rav has his ideas, and I have mine. Many years ago, when we first came to Los Angeles, I wanted to build a proper Centre, but we had nowhere near the kind of money we needed to do so. The Rav warned me, "You're biting off more than you can chew. I feel it's better to build the Centre gradually."

"But a gradual approach is not better." I argued.

He insisted it was.

And round and round we went. But in the end, we found the money to build the Centre the way it should be built. It still exists today, of course, and is thriving.

Although we differed completely over the right approach to take, we shared the same goal, which was ultimately to create a beautiful space for The Kabbalah Centre in Los Angeles. And as it turned out, my sense of urgency, coupled with the Rav's desire to build with care, created the best possible outcome. In an interdependent relationship, you may not always agree on the means, but you are in overall agreement about the ultimate goal. Your values and aspirations are aligned.

This kind of relationship requires two people who are spiritually mature enough to stand on their own two feet. So the first question you should ask yourself is, "Do I have that level of maturity myself?" If you don't, then you have some work to do. This book will help. As you study the tenets of Kabbalistic wisdom and apply them in your life, you will become increasingly connected to the Light. The Light is the source of everything, and when it enters your life, you will no longer feel the need to lean on someone else.

If your partner has not reached this level of maturity, then you may be in for a wild ride. You need somebody on your wavelength so that you can love him for who and what he is, not for who you hope he'll become. If you're in a relationship in which there is this kind of incompatibility, however, I am not suggesting that you end it. Kabbalah provides tools to work with every situation in your life, however difficult it may be.

On the other hand, if you are about to begin a new relationship, try to see the person as he truly is. If you observe a prospective partner clearly without projecting your own wishes and desires onto him, you will know whether you should avoid the relationship and thus spare yourself a lot of heartache. This is not as easy as it sounds. We all live in the world of Malchut, where we are readily seduced by appearances.

8

Tikune:
The Correction Tool

Each time we surrender to our reactive behavior and fail to practice restriction, we have to make a correction. Kabbalah calls this tikune, a term referring to the part of ourselves that we need to work on in this Lifetime.

The fact of the matter is, most of us come into this world with at least some baggage from our previous lifetimes. We have these little jealousies, these petty hatreds, this sense of entitlement or intolerance. We didn't master them? Not quite? Okay, back we come to work through them again.

Each time we surrender to our reactive behavior and fail to practice restriction, we have to make a correction. Kabbalah calls this *tikune*, a term referring to the part of ourselves that we need to work on in this lifetime. Your particular *tikune* is everything you do when you follow the path of least resistance, as this path is usually made up of self-centered bad habits. You can have a *tikune* with money, health, career, or any other area in your life. It is in relationships, however, that you will experience your *tikune* most strongly. As you learn to become conscious of your reactive nature and to restrict it, you are pursuing your ultimate purpose in life. This is nothing less than reconnection with the Light and the experience of joy that comes from it.

One sure sign that you are coming up against your *tikune* is the feeling of emotional discomfort. Indeed, all the people and situations in your life that truly bother you are merely participants in your process of correction. A spiritual way to look at this is to see that everything you currently consider a problem is in reality an opportunity that the Light has sent you. If you find yourself in a difficult relationship with your partner, it's because you have something to learn from him and he has something to learn from you.

When you have this perspective on life, it shifts the way you relate to loved ones. You become more tolerant and less inclined to judge or criticize them. You realize that the difficulties and obstacles they appear to create are without exception opportunities for you to grow spiritually. Indeed, the Light has sent you these people in order to help you change your nature and become unconditionally sharing. When you do manage to change in this way, the aggravating situation often clears up spontaneously. If action is required, then the Light acts through you, and your response to the person tends to create unity and healing.

The movie *Groundhog Day*, starring Bill Murray, provides a funny but accurate depiction of the principle of *tikune*. Bill Murray plays Phil Connors, a weatherman who is the ultimate reactive character, consumed by his own self-indulgence, arrogance, and indifference to the world around him. Phil gets stuck in a time warp. He is trapped in February 2—Groundhog Day. The same day keeps repeating itself over and over again, and no one knows it but him.

This is great fun at first. Phil takes advantage of the situation, learning all he can about Punxsutawney, Pennsylvania, and the people in it so as to manipulate them and serve his own self-interest. But his life turns into a nightmare when the momentary pleasures wear off and not a drop of lasting fulfillment is to be found.

Pushed to suicide, Phil Connors awakens morning after morning to find himself in the same town confronting the same events. There is no escape—not even death. Finally, after enduring tremendous suffering, he decides to change himself because he discovers that there is no joy in trying to change the world around him. So he begins to perform good deeds and to help the people who are experiencing the same misfortunes each day.

Suddenly, he feels true fulfillment. Inspired by this Light, he goes on a rampage of sharing all over the town, winning the hearts of everyone. Eventually he winds up with the girl of his dreams, and the nightmare ends. He has broken the recurring cycle and finds himself in a brand new day, arm in arm with his true soulmate.

If your life seems like *Groundhog Day* and you keep experiencing the same relationship challenges repeatedly, it is because you haven't yet seen that your relationships are not the real problem. You keep attracting the same type of person or situation into your life because there is something in *you* that needs to change. When you make the inner change that is required of you, your outer world will shift automatically. You won't have the same experiences anymore. You'll attract different people and situations into your life.

9

The Positive of the Negative:
The Conflict Tool

Ask yourself whether insisting on getting your way is really worth all the hurt and misery it's causing.

A few years ago, Joan Osborne sang a popular song with the words "What if God was one of us?" Can you imagine what a difference it would make if you could always keep in mind the presence of God within your spouse? Would you get angry with him or dislike him if you truly knew that by doing so you were losing your temper with the Creator? Of course not. You might try to justify your actions by pointing out your husband's faults, but recognize that when you hurt another person, you are in reality hurting yourself. At that moment, you are actually distancing yourself from the Creator.

If you look more closely at the emotions and actions that disconnect you from others, you will see that they are expressions of selfish behavior. Kabbalah refers to this as the Desire to Receive for the Self Alone. What is anger? Is it rage that he didn't hear *me*, that he didn't appreciate *my needs*? Jealousy and hatred come from the same place. They are self-inflicted emotions, so we are responsible for the pain they cause us.

What is your punishment if you are envious, angry, jealous, or hurtful? Envy, anger, jealousy, or hurtfulness. Think of how painful these states are. What greater deterrent to being negative and spiteful could there be than to experience these feelings? If you continue to hurt yourself with these emotions, it is because you persist in blaming others for your reactions. But others are never at fault. They are merely messengers showing you what you need to learn about yourself.

When you see your partner in this light, you appreciate the essential oneness that lies beneath your surface differences, and you become grateful to him for providing you with an extraordinary opportunity to grow spiritually. You are not two distinct individuals. You are, in fact, a single unit or soul—the male and female aspect, Adam and Eve—working on a common project. Once you grasp this, the energy in your relationship shifts from competition to collaboration. Now you and your partner can begin to work together to clear away the negativities that separate you from each other and from the Light.

This new goal of spiritual union helps you overcome all obstacles. You may have areas of serious incompatibility, but if you make a sincere decision to work to attain higher levels of consciousness together, you will eventually have a wonderful relationship.

* * *

Every relationship generates conflict from time to time; it's inevitable. However, conflicts take on an entirely different meaning when seen from the perspective of your *tikune*. You can even learn to welcome them and be grateful for them. So when the next relationship challenge surfaces, try to take yourself out of the situation for just a moment. Don't respond in your usual manner; just listen to your inner voice and ask yourself what you could do right now to change the movie you're in, to break out of your own personal *Groundhog Day*. Chances are you will be told, and you will begin to see why the situation is happening and how it can serve you and your partner.

If you do not yet have this understanding—if it is too difficult to hear that inner voice—just remember that determining who is "right" in an argument and who is "wrong" is unimportant. What matters is that you take sole responsibility for stopping the conflict. If you find this difficult to do, ask yourself whether insisting on getting your way is really worth all the hurt and misery it's causing. Sometimes all it takes is a short pause to allow time for a little common sense to appear. If you manage to shift your perspective and really become interested in helping your partner, it will be impossible for the conflict to continue as the Light enters your interactions.

Relationships need to be nourished in this manner, with effort and attention. Always work on your ego. Find at least one place in an argument where your mate is right. See if you can stop the dispute before it destroys the love between you. This means restricting your impulsive reactions and rising above them. When you do this, you will often find that the situation is quickly resolved even if your partner doesn't cooperate. In fact, you need not insist on a team effort. Do your part, and in most cases you will be amazed at how readily your partner responds to you.

Why does this happen? Think back to the light bulb metaphor I used earlier. Your effort to restrict allows the energy of the Creator to enter into this physical world and into the specific situation. At that moment, it matters little if your partner is initially uncooperative. He contains a spark of the Creator as well, and your genuine act of sharing will touch him, causing the situation to inevitably soften and allowing for the Light to emerge.

A relationship acts as a mirror in which you can—if you choose to look at your reflection honestly—see your own negativity and move to correct it. Every painful moment in your life contains a lesson. If your husband comes home in a bad mood and starts picking on you, consider it from the soul's point of view. Instead of snapping at him with a reactive, "What's your problem?" look for the lesson you are asked to learn. Is this about patience? Understanding? Tolerance? Generosity? Or is there some other quality you need to develop?

You may not recognize it immediately, but you can be sure that your partner's behavior contains a lesson. If you work at trying to understand, you will eventually discover what you are being asked to learn. Even if your husband has traits that need changing—he's genuinely inconsiderate or unhelpful—become conscious of your ego reactions to the situation. When we feel we are the object of clearly unacceptable behavior, we generally tend to push, push, push. The unfortunate result is that we actually push our partner in the opposite direction. It's like making a child eat rice pudding. To this day, I won't touch the stuff because my mother forced it down my throat when I was a kid. A similar process can occur in relationships. Rather than backing off and allowing your partner to grow—and working on yourself so that he is inspired by the changes in you—you may try to use subtle forms of coercion. These efforts are certain to turn your partner off and can blow up in your face.

People do not react well to being manipulated. When you know that your husband has returned from a business meeting and he's upset, take your ego out of the situation and let him express himself. Don't bombard him with your needs immediately. Bide your time until the right opportunity presents itself, and then step into it. If an argument is brewing, say to yourself, "Okay, you know what? I can be generous here. I'm just going to listen and not disagree immediately. I'll give Sam the space to vent emotionally. Later we can look at the situation from other viewpoints."

Find a way to have a different kind of conversation—one in which compassion prevails over anger. When you're hurt, it's easy to blow it out of proportion and slide straight into rage. But if you can exercise enough willpower to postpone the discussion until later—perhaps over a quiet dinner in a calm location—you may find that many of your difficulties miraculously vanish, and those that remain are often easily resolved.

It's easy to get stuck in a marital rut. But if you recognize that relationship conflict is a valuable mechanism that points out where you need to evolve, you need not despair.

When you become accustomed to observing your reactive nature, you will be able to restrict it more consistently. This process of restriction reconnects a circuit, as though you had literally switched the Light on in your life. When you open yourself up to the Light, you come closer to its energy, and that energy gives you the creative force to achieve transformation.

You don't have to go looking for the Light, because it is always on. The ever-present energy of the Creator is yours to tap into anytime you wish. You need only go inside yourself and draw it out. Then you will shine with the Light of the Creator, and your life and your relationships will shine as well.

10

What Your Therapist Is Too Well Paid to Tell You: The Criticism Tool

—

Your partner's criticism of you

is rarely arbitrary.

He may not be conscious of what

he is doing, but he will be

pointing out aspects of your behavior

that genuinely need correction.

What goes hand in hand with conflict? Why, criticism, of course. If you're fighting with your loved one, you can be sure that criticism, whether overt or implied, is in the air between you.

We all hate to be criticized, yet we are usually quick to pounce on others. But when you're the one under fire, resist the temptation to retaliate. Instead, think hard about what your partner is saying. Perhaps he's expressing himself in angry or vengeful tones. Still, that doesn't mean there's no truth in his observations.

Your partner's criticism of you is rarely arbitrary. He may not be conscious of what he's doing, but he will be pointing out aspects of your behavior that genuinely need correction. If you can refrain from getting upset and really listen to the message, you'll receive a powerful lesson. When this happens, you, your partner, and your relationship will all benefit—which is quite a bargain.

Although criticism can be beneficial to you, I recommend that you refrain from criticizing others unless they ask you to do so. Sometimes, however, it is clearly necessary to correct someone, and *The Bible* gives a beautiful recommendation about how and when to do this. If you see someone doing something wrong and you wish to correct them, three conditions need to be fulfilled before you say anything:

1. Your criticism must be true.
2. You must love the other person genuinely and sincerely.
3. You must know that he will listen.

If you are honest about your own behavior, you may see that most of the time you don't follow these rules. Your criticism is really more about your own needs than it is about the other person. As you learn to become a truly giving person, however, you will become sensitive to the needs of others and to what will truly benefit them, and your corrections will then be of service to them.

If you feel that you are becoming judgmental with your partner, try countering it by practicing the art of listening. As I've suggested in the Listening Tool, put yourself in your husband's shoes—ask the Light for help in this—and try to understand what motivates him. When you can get inside his skin and feel his pain or anxiety, you can become a friend.

What should you do if your partner hurts your feelings? It's important to address the issue with him, but again, do so in a loving way. If you approach him in anger, it will create a veil between you. Sometimes this means you will have to wait before discussing the problem in order to give your anger time to subside. This can be hard, because your emotions will try to push you into speaking. But recognize that your reactive nature is operating, and see if you can restrict it.

Once you have reconnected with your sharing nature and the Light is flowing through you again, you can come to your partner with love and say, "You know what? When you answered me so abruptly before, you hurt me. Our relationship is very important to me, so could you please take more care next time?" This helps draw back the veils that separate you, allowing you to experience genuine compassion and intimacy.

We once had a volunteer at The Kabbalah Centre in Los Angeles whose behavior shows how criticism can be used in both a destructive and a loving way. Sidney was a strong, successful, domineering sort of man. His wife, Nicole, appeared to be a perfect match for him because she had a submissive personality. He would take charge of everything, big and small, and most of the time she would go along with whatever he proposed. Although Sidney told me in private that he wanted his wife to assert herself more, it was clear that he was unconsciously controlling his wife, using his power to feel good about himself. It appealed to him that she consistently put his needs and wishes first. "I encourage her to be more assertive," he complained. "I tell her she should stand up on her own two feet. But she thinks I'm criticizing her, and she gets defensive."

Little wonder. I'd heard the two of them interacting, and I knew that the way he urged her to become more independent was neither loving nor compassionate. It felt downright judgmental and hurtful. "Are you sure you really want her to be more assertive?" I asked.

"What do you mean?"

"Well, it seems to me that you're not truly ready to give up control." At first Sidney resisted the suggestion that he take some responsibility for the situation. But since there was no proper exchange in the relationship, it eventually became so unfulfilling that even Sidney realized he had no choice but to look in the mirror and see what needed changing in himself. So he examined his motives and eventually recognized what he was doing. Then, to his credit, he made a concerted effort to work on himself.

Rather than always coming from a self-centered, hurtful place, Sidney began to make comments that were motivated by concern for Nicole and for the well-being of their marriage. He genuinely encouraged her to come into her own power. He worked hard on restricting his tendency to run the relationship, and if he saw Nicole fall into a pattern of compliance with him, he would bring it to her attention.

Once I observed them choosing a movie to watch that evening. Nicole instinctively deferred to him. "Whatever you want is fine with me," she said in her habitual way.

But Sidney was able to say with real kindness, "You know, honey, if there's a movie you'd prefer to watch, I'd really like you to tell me. In fact, whenever there's something important to you, I'd feel a lot better if you'd tell me clearly what you want."

Before, had he suggested that she make a choice about something, she would have heard it as a put-down, which indeed it would have been. Now, however, she could detect a real note of caring in him, and that made all the difference. Each time he genuinely worked at building up Nicole, he grew, and he gave her the space to come into her own power.

Nicole was a talented artist. When she began to think of putting on a small exhibition, Sidney was helpful and supportive. The show was a real success.

As Nicole started returning the nurturing and support to her husband that she'd received from him, Sidney's life became more fulfilling than he'd ever thought possible. Their marriage improved immeasurably.

11

Dealing with Loss:
The Endings Tool

Separation from a loved one,
as painful as it might be,
is often the jolt you need to free
your spirit and rekindle your
awareness of your need to grow.

The ending of a relationship through death is one of the most painful events in life. When you lose a mate, you feel your world has caved in. It's more devastating than any other loss, save that of a child.

Your pain can make you lose perspective. It may push you to buy into a belief in a fundamental disconnectedness among people. It may even cause you to question the Creator. "If God is all good," you may ask, "why is there suffering in the world? Why do people become sick? Why do they die? Where's the humanity, the Light in that?"

I have a friend who has a serious condition with poor circulation. Until Paul was diagnosed with this problem, he was fine. He was a caring man who practiced the art of sharing. The minute this potentially fatal medical condition came to light, however, he locked himself in his home, railing at God. Instead of recognizing this illness as an opportunity to repay his karmic debt and grow, he reacted in a way that blocked healing. You could say that Paul kicked over the full milk bucket. "I was a pious man all my life," he complained. "I studied, I taught my children. Why has God forsaken me in this way?"

Paul's situation reminds me of Rabbi Akiva. Captured by his enemies, he was to be flayed alive the next day. His student came to him that evening and asked, "Dear teacher, how are they going to do this terrible thing to you? Where is God?"

But Rabbi Akiva replied, "Go away snake. All my life I've been waiting for the opportunity all my life, and now I'm not going to shy away and ask, 'Why has God abandoned me?' " For Paul as well as this Sage, the test is in our reaction to the suffering.

In the eye of God, there is no time, space, or motion. The Light He has sent here in the form of a soul must eventually return to the Creator. That soul will have learned its lesson and completed its process. This is the way of the world of Malchut, the world in which we live. So even though most women have "separation issues," at the soul level there is no such thing as separation. This is just not true, even in death. We are all one.

I know this may be difficult to accept, but if you remember that we are all on a spiritual journey and that death is just one part of that journey, perhaps you can see how the same principles apply to this most tragic kind of loss.

What is true for death can also be true during separation and divorce. Your soul knows that events occur for a purpose, and it doesn't try to hold on when the circumstances of a relationship begin a natural process of change. It realizes that this physical separation from the one you love is exactly what you need to stimulate your growth, and it knows that your partner's growth will be enhanced as well. This is evident when a spouse or a lover dies, but it's also true when a loved one leaves.

If you become anxious because someone you love is moving away from you, this is not the response of your soul but rather that of your emotional self. Of course, I'm not suggesting that it is inappropriate to grieve or to experience heartache. These are natural feelings that arise when you lose someone close to you. However, it's difficult to grow spiritually when you're stuck in a rut carved out of habitual reactive behavior.

Separation from a loved one, as painful as it may be, is often the jolt you need to free your spirit and rekindle your awareness of your need to grow. From your soul's perspective, you're fortunate when a driving force appears from above that removes you from your comfort zone. When a separation occurs, the first thing to look at is the "me" that's suffering. This self-examination allows you to view the situation from a more elevated place. Remember that the players in your drama appear the way they do to teach you a lesson. It's hard to look this truth in the eye; when the chips are down, you're likely to run back into your old ways of thinking.

Especially in cases of separation and divorce, it's much easier to find fault with your spouse or lover than to be thankful for the opportunity you've been given. But ask yourself:

- "What am I to learn from this ordeal? What is the life lesson I am to absorb?"

- "What's the debt I'm paying back to the universe?"

- "If this is happening to me, then how am I responsible for what I'm going through? What role do I play in this drama?"

If it is not immediately evident to you what your lesson, debt, or role is, say to yourself, *"Maybe my spirit needs to grow a little more, and then I will understand."* Be patient with yourself.

If you are insecure, you may feel you are not good enough to hang onto your relationship. Perhaps you unconsciously assume that your partner will abandon you when he awakens and recognizes who you *really* are. Should he leave, the pain of the separation will be especially intense because it will stimulate tender feelings already connected to your negative self-image. If this is your situation, understand that we are all put here with a self-image of one kind or another, and that the whole job of our being in this world is to elevate ourselves above it. As unpleasant as separation may be, it can be an extremely powerful medicine.

As you act out the play that you have staged with your mate, remember that we are all clay in the Potter's hand. He has put us in exactly the right place at exactly the right time so that we may eventually fulfill our destinies. When you see the truth of this, it becomes easier to forgive a partner who you feel has wronged you. After all, if he is simply playing his role to perfection, what is there really to forgive?

12

I Accept My Apology:
The Forgiveness Tool

—

The essence of forgiveness lies in understanding that there is really nothing to forgive. No one has harmed you, nor can they ever harm you. Everything is a reminder to let go and trust God.

You may think you are a forgiving person, but your forgiveness might be only intellectual. You say, "He hurt me, but I forgive him anyway." This is not the deepest forgiveness you can experience.

When someone harms you in any way, your first instinct will typically be to get even. If you harbor this feeling, you'll want revenge whenever you think about this person, despite the fact that you might be a paragon of virtue elsewhere in your life and may behave toward the rest of the world with the utmost kindness and goodness.

One of my students, Jennifer, was furious with her estranged husband. In her estimation, Rick had drained their bank accounts and had taken more than his fair share of their money when he had moved out. Her first thought was, "He stole from me, but I'll get back at him. I'll hire an attorney and take him to the cleaners." Already, in that thought, dark forces were at work.

"Hang on a minute, Jennifer," I said. Why don't you try changing your script to: *"If Rick took my money, then I had to lose it, so I must work harder to follow the path of the Light, and the Light will take care of me."*

Jennifer looked at me sharply and asked, "Well, why did I have to lose the money?"

"This is not about punishment," I explained. "It's really about the perfection of creation. Nothing happens randomly or without reason. Perhaps you owe Rick money from a past life, or maybe in the past you took something from someone and the time has come for you to experience how that feels. Maybe this isn't about money at all, but about something else you need to learn. If that's the case, you'll eventually get the money back, because you can't lose something that is truly yours. I suggest that you say to yourself, 'The Creator, in His infinite perfect sharing, allowed this to happen in order to help me transform. So what would He like me to learn?' "

"But still," Jennifer stammered, "you don't think I should just let it go, do you?"

"No," I replied. "I'm just pointing out that everything has a reason. If you accept responsibility for your own reactions to what has happened —which is not at all the same thing as accepting blame or feeling guilty—you will see what lesson you need to learn."

Jennifer eventually did look at her situation in this way, and she recognized how angry she was with Rick for leaving her. Her rage actually had nothing to do with the money. Instead, she felt disrespected, unappreciated, and, above all, betrayed. However, she began to see that she was the person who had created these feelings. Certainly Rick appeared to have done her an injustice, but he couldn't *make* Jennifer have the feelings she was experiencing. Her reaction was something she could control.

Once Jennifer looked at her reactions without blaming her ex-husband, she noticed the pattern underlying her feelings of rejection: Her father had been cold and distant, and she never felt that he had truly loved her. These insights caused her to start moving in a more spiritual direction in her life. A few months later, she admitted to me that Rick had inadvertently done her a great service by leaving, since it pushed her to examine her own life.

By the way, Jennifer did have her day in court, and Rick did return some of the money. But that wasn't the point. Her suffering and sense of financial loss were incidental to the Light's real purpose, which was to give Jennifer the opportunity to grow.

* * *

When it comes to forgiveness, everything you experience is a test. When you become stuck in an unforgiving posture, you have not yet learned the lesson. The essence of forgiveness lies in understanding that there is really nothing to forgive. No one has harmed you, nor can they ever harm you. Everything is a reminder to let go and trust God. Other people never truly hurt you; you hurt yourself by disconnecting from the Light Force. Everything negative in our lives is designed to help us remember this fact.

Of course, this doesn't mean you should lie back and allow others to step all over you. On the contrary. When you bring Light into your actions, you will become effective. But don't hold onto the past or carry a grudge. If you are stuck in what has happened to you, you become resentful, unhappy, pessimistic, and embittered. Who are the shining, youthful people you know? They're the ones who are in love with life because they know how to let go of the past and move on.

In this age, with its quickening pace, it is of the utmost importance that you set an intention to leave all the old garbage behind. Try to wash yourself clean of the injustices you feel others have done you. Emotional scars block your Godliness from you. Say goodbye to them so that you can jump into the bright future that awaits you.

* * *

Of course, along with the need to forgive, you may also need to be forgiven. How many injustices have you committed toward others? An intriguing Jewish law states that in the time of *Elul*—in the month of Virgo—you should approach people whom you've hurt during the year and ask their pardon. You know how quickly you resent those who have hurt you, so be patient with those from whom you seek forgiveness. If they refuse to accept your apology after three genuine attempts, however, you can appeal to the Creator to forgive your action.

The Bible tells us that Jacob ran away from his brother Esau to live with Laban, who was soon to be his father-in-law, because he had deceived his father Isaac and had stolen the blessing rightly belonging to Esau. When Jacob asked his mother, Rebecca, when he should return, she replied, "Until your brother's fury subsides—until your brother's anger against you subsides—and he forgets what you have done to him." Kabbalah tells us that by this she meant that once you have removed all your own destructive thoughts about another, you can receive a clean slate from the Creator.

The universe is a mirror, reflecting back to you everything you put into it. If you want to use a painful experience such as divorce to help you grow, you must see the event as it truly is—as a lesson, not a punishment. When you learn the lesson, you are relieved of the suffering, and Light and joy can come flooding back into your life once more.

13

I Can See Clearly Now:
The Honesty Tool

If you're not truly honest with yourself,
you'll spend the rest of your life
trying to fix other people,
but they are never the real problem.

Some people believe they're being dishonest if they don't immediately express every little hurt they feel. When I suggest that you forgive others and refrain from judging and criticizing them, I'm not saying that you should deny your emotions. Sadly, however, when people express their hurt feelings, they usually do so angrily. They come from a destructive frame of mind, not one in which they are hoping to create a positive outcome from the difficulty.

Then, of course, there are those instances in which we are not being totally honest with a loved one out of our own self-interest or because we're deluding ourselves. I have a Hawaiian friend, Gary, who once confided to me that he was hiding something from his partner. He sought my advice. "I have a savings account containing several hundred thousand dollars," he told me. "But I keep it hidden from Mila." "Why did you do that?" I asked him.

"She's a spendthrift," he replied matter-of-factly. "It's as simple as that. She'd run through that money in a year if she found out about it. I know it's not great that I've been dishonest with her, but telling her the truth doesn't seem a good solution either."

"Well, why are you in a relationship with a woman you don't trust?" I asked.

From his wrinkled brow, I could tell that my question perplexed Gary.

"Look," I continued, "you're wondering how wise it is to let Mila know about your money. That means you don't trust her. If that's the case, then you have far bigger issues to deal with than that secret slush fund. And if you believe she's too foolish to know about it, it's you who are the fool. Why are you with her anyway, if you feel that way about her?"

As our conversation continued, it became clear that there was indeed more to the situation than the money. To begin with, Gary was not married to Mila, and he was afraid to commit to her. He saw the bank account as his escape fund. In addition, having deceived her for such a long time, he was afraid to finally reveal the truth. "She'll be so angry with me when she finds out, I'm sure she'll leave me," he declared. Gary found himself in a weird situation. He didn't want to move forward into a truly honest and committed union, but he also didn't want Mila to go, even though the relationship obviously couldn't grow and develop, having been built on such a faulty foundation.

"Honesty is a quality of the Light," I counseled. "If you want to be the Light in the relationship, you have to be yourself. But in truth, you're living a lie. I'm not saying concealment isn't appropriate at times, but you are hiding things out of fear and insecurity, and that's never a good motivation."

As we spoke, Gary saw that his deceit was driving a wedge into his relationship and that he needed to be truthful with Mila. A few days later, he took a plane back to Hawaii with the intention of speaking plainly to his girlfriend and accepting whatever consequences ensued.

Recently, Gary returned to California and related the rest of the story to me. Not surprisingly, Mila had initially been shocked. But she recovered and was able to appreciate his honesty and courage in stepping forward with the truth. Unfortunately, this period of understanding was short-lived. Soon, she slipped back into a state of recrimination and resentment. Their relationship collapsed, and Gary had by then returned to California to start a new life.

"Well, how do you feel about how things turned out?" I asked him.

"I'm fine with it now," he admitted. "Confessing about the money brought out the truth about our relationship. I guess I was afraid to know the truth, but now I'm glad I do. It's a relief."

Honesty generally does require the sort of courage Gary exhibited. When we hesitate to tell the truth, it is often because we are afraid of the consequences. Sometimes, as in Gary's case, we're afraid for good reason. Even if the initial reaction to our honesty is messy, however, it is sometimes better to let a shaky structure collapse. That way, we allow room for a more solid and authentic relationship to take its place.

The kind of honesty Gary demonstrated is likely to become an option for you when you stop blaming others for your experiences. They are never the real problem. There are no negative husbands or lovers. Your loved ones also have within them a spark of the Light Force of the Creator. They are here to help you complete your correction process. When you stop trying to fix them and instead look closely to see what needs fixing within you, you'll make a breakthrough in any situation, however much it may appear that your partner is responsible for it.

It may not always be easy to recognize what needs correcting, because your negative aspects may be concealed in your blind spot. You may thus need help in detecting them. If you have a close friend whom you trust, ask where he or she thinks your veils are. Perhaps you argue simply for the sake of argument. Or maybe you're self-centered or insensitive. Let them reveal these aspects to you. You will be amazed at the power of honest appraisal and self-appraisal. They will enable you to speak the truth and to deal charitably with others.

* * *

But what is truth? It's not something obvious. My truth and your truth are not the same. Each one of us sees what our senses allow us to see, which creates differences—sometimes minor, sometimes major—in what we consider the truth. Believe it or not, there are times when lying is an acceptable practice. For instance, if you don't want to tell your husband about something that occurred during the day because you know it will upset him, according to spiritual law you don't have to tell him. You can be economical with the truth for the purpose of making peace in your home. When you tell a white lie in this context, it is permissible.

Moreover, if telling the truth means hurting someone unnecessarily, you remember those childhood taunts like *"You're ugly and your mother dresses you funny"*, then it is better not to be truthful. The conscious person—the one who is really working on transforming herself—will ask, "Is it necessary for me to make this statement?" Your partner may ask, for instance, "Do you like my new tie?" The truth is that you don't, but you might sense the need to reply, "It's okay," or "Sure," so that you don't hurt him. However, if he's asking you because he's uncertain about how it goes with his suit (and what impression that will make on his new boss) and he really needs your honest opinion, then of course you should be truthful.

Unfortunately, sometimes being brutally honest is really a covert way of hurting your partner rather than being constructive. Deep down you actually intend to inflict injury. If you come from a place of real sharing, however, you will know when it's better to tell a little white lie than to tell the cold truth.

Of course, I'm not advocating the introduction of lies and dishonesty into a relationship. That would obviously erode trust and ruin your chances for a happy life together. Rather, I am talking about being truly loving. In your heart of hearts, you always know what's helpful in a situation and what's harmful. That is the essence of honesty—being truthful about your own motives.

This might sound complex, but it is not. Gary, my friend from Hawaii, just needed to be nudged a little to see that there was a lot more to his story than Mila's spendthrift ways. If you make it a point to be honest with yourself, then you'll know whether you're acting and speaking from a loving heart or trying to gain an unfair advantage over someone. It's not difficult, provided that you're straight with yourself.

Honesty allowed Gary to identify the hidden negativities that were directing his behavior. Common sense tells us that you can control only what you can see. Once he acknowledged that fear was motivating him, Gary was able to restrict his behavior. Then the Light was able to come into his life, and clarity could govern his relationship to the benefit of all involved.

14

Guilt is a Four-Letter Word: The Self-Responsibility Tool

Self-responsibility and guilt are not the same thing. Self-responsibility is liberating, whereas guilt is generally a trap that keeps you stuck.

King David was traveling on a road when a man named Caspi began yelling and cursing at him. The king's men wanted to protect their monarch, so they jumped into action and began beating Caspi. But King David intervened. "No." he ordered his men. "Stop. If this man is cursing me, then I am worthy of being cursed." The wise king knew the truth: I must deserve these curses in some way.

The next time someone causes you a great deal of stress, just think about why this energy is coming to you. I am not proposing that you feel guilty. Self-responsibility and guilt are not the same thing. Self-responsibility is liberating, whereas guilt is generally a trap that keeps you stuck.

You might find it relatively easy to take responsibility for your relationships. I hope this book helps you see that you are never a victim and that you can always change what you experience, even with an unwilling partner. However, you may feel more resistant toward taking responsibility for other aspects of your life, such as your physical health.

Why do we get sick? Sometimes illness is the body's way of telling us to slow down. We push ourselves too hard, and the body needs a chance to rest. Sometimes we become ill as a way to gain attention. Generally, when we're ill, negative thoughts and actions have disconnected us from the Light and have caused us to lose our protective shield. We then become extremely vulnerable to disease. A sense of guilt about this is not helpful, however, since it just creates more negativity. In fact, guilt is often an excuse not to do anything about the situation. Self-responsibility, on the other hand, means that you take charge of your life and use everything that happens to you in a way that promotes your spiritual growth.

Of course, when children are sick or are born with defects, it is hard for us to accept. How can a little child be responsible for his or her pain and suffering? The assumption behind this question is that we know what is good and bad in life. In reality, however, we usually have it all backwards. What we interpret as a "punishment from God" may actually be a very privileged set of circumstances, a gift. Even if a child is born with a severe physical handicap, it is not necessarily a negative.

A holy man had a mentally disabled child who was dying. He came to his teacher and asked, "What did I do wrong to have this child?"

"You mean, what did you do right to have this child?" his teacher replied. "Children like this are special souls who have very little left to do in this world," he continued. "They ask to come down in a body in which they will create little negativity so that when they return to the Source, they are as pure as possible."

This story has particular poignancy in my family because my grandson was born with Down's syndrome. My son and daughter-in-law, far from seeing this as a form of punishment, appreciate his life as a special blessing and view his presence in their household as a gift.

In fact, shortly after my own daughter was born, it was clear that she had a problem with her legs. The doctors thought she suffered from cerebral palsy or muscular dystrophy, so they put her in a cast for two years. We then went to see a new specialist. He told us, "Doctors diagnose, but God gives the prognosis." So he took off the cast, and within a month, little Suri was standing on her toes. In a year she was walking normally. This new specialist did Grand Rounds with my daughter, and when the other doctors asked him why he was showing them a normal child, he whipped out her medical history. It's all given to us to learn from. Perhaps I wasn't attentive enough as a mother, and that was the lesson I needed to learn.

Make an effort to see the good in every situation and to appreciate negative events as opportunities rather than punishments. Your actions do have consequences, but you're also free to change your actions and thus change what you experience. Guilt and shame block you from taking true responsibility for your life. They put you in the role of victim and make you feel powerless, so that you become an effect rather than a cause.

People have every kind of excuse for the bad state of their lives, but the truth of the matter is that a soul is put into a situation that provides the ideal conditions for it to do its job, whatever that may be. When we take full responsibility for ourselves, we become aligned with cosmic forces that are intent on helping us grow.

15

Be Happy or Else:
The Cheerfulness Tool

Just as environmentally unfriendly products damage the ozone layer, so do spiritually unhealthy thoughts harm your aura, your metaphysical shield.

If you can see the universe as a friendly presence (which it is), then you can lighten up, literally. Not only will your intimate relationships improve, but your interactions with everyone you meet—in restaurants and stores, at school or on the street, at home or at work—will become warm and courteous.

What happens if you don't thank your waitress for bringing you a glass of water? What happens when you fail to smile or say hello to a shop assistant? Your egocentric attitude limits your pleasure in life. Do you want to participate in filling the world with sad, scowling faces? A woman who arises in the morning and is grouchy has woken up to the knowledge that she'll have a miserable day. How could it be otherwise?

Unfortunately, the people to whom you are closest are often the ones to whom you present your glum side. You might be all smiles at the grocery store but may turn into a grouch the minute you step over the threshold of your front door. This is a sign of complacency—a terribly corrosive force in any intimate relationship. Recognize that your low moods are part of your reactive nature, and make an effort to stop them. Again, this is not a question of repressing your legitimate feelings. Just become aware of the habitual negativities that arise when you are with your mate, and make an effort to restrict them. Restriction invites the Light back into your life, and when this happens, your mood naturally elevates.

If you are challenged in this area or have difficulty smiling and being cheerful, try a simple remedy. First, become aware of the way you interact with others during the day. It's only when you notice your negative states that you can do something about them. Then remind yourself to smile even though you may not feel like it. If you do this, you'll notice that your mood improves and that it becomes easier to continue smiling.

Of course, in order to feel motivated to try this little exercise, you must first recognize the value of smiling. It is not just something superficial and dispensable. Smiles and laughter bring Light into your life; they lift your burdens and reduce stress and anxiety. Smiling people radiate a different kind of energy than do those who are gloomy. And they actually feel happier, even if what they're doing requires a conscious effort. There are even health benefits to smiling. Studies in kinesiology (a system that tests the muscles' reactions to different stimuli) show that when a person thinks a negative thought, the muscle being tested actually becomes weaker, whereas when the thought is positive, the muscle remains strong.

If you're negative, your immune system is depressed. A huge, dark hole forms in you that attracts disease, both physical and mental. Just as environmentally unfriendly products damage the ozone layer, so do spiritually unhealthy thoughts harm your aura, your metaphysical shield. When you're angry or envious, you create little pinholes in your aura. As these holes multiply or enlarge, your resistance runs down, and you fall prey to the darkness.

Depression, the most widespread psychological disorder in our society, is one example of the effects of this darkness. It is a direct result of disconnection from the Light. The cure, naturally, is reconnection. If you re-create the circuit by using the simple technique I've described, the Light will shine through you, and your mind and body will be much healthier.

In the same way, you can receive protection from heart disease, cancer, and other major killers. There is a direct correlation between your health and the amount of Light in your life. Smiling might seem like a frill, especially in today's challenging world, but it is no small thing.

Your smile sends out the message: *My heart is open to be a friend, to listen to you, to have empathy for you. Inside of me I have made room for you.*

This triggers a domino effect in the world. When you smile, you stimulate others to extend beyond themselves and to enter a world in which they share with others and others share with them. Conversely, when you are anxious or fearful, you elicit these states in those around you, encouraging others to be limited and self-concerned.

The Chinese say, "When we were born, we cried while all around us laughed. Let us live our lives so that when we leave this world, we can laugh while all around us cry." Try to cultivate a smiling, cheerful attitude. Life is a wonderful dance, and you can enjoy it even more if you tread lightly.

16

Keep the Light On:
The Sex Tool

*The purpose of the sexual act is
to bring down Light——love,
if you will——into the world by
creating circular energy.*

Many people believe intercourse is simply a form of self-gratification or physical release, and they conduct their relationships on that basis. But I think it's important to look at the deeper meaning of sex.

The purpose of the sexual act is to bring down Light—love, if you will—into the world by creating circular energy. During sex, a circuit is created in which you and your lover divinely intertwine with the Light Force. Just as in our metaphorical light bulb, a filament connects the positive and negative poles, and when the electrical current flows, the bulb sparkles. You and your partner are no longer simply two bodies— you become one, united in physical, emotional, and spiritual realms.

When a child is conceived in relationships with this kind of circularity, she is conceived in love, and she'll have fewer challenges in life. This is especially true if she is conceived at a prime spiritual moment, such as Friday evening after midnight. This is when God enters *Gan Eden*, the valley of the angels—the place of perfect peace and unity. The purest of souls sit around God there and watch the couples who are uniting out of pure love. God turns to one of the little waiting souls and asks, "Is that where you'd like to be?" If so, this is the point at which that soul incarnates.

The fact that sex is designed to bring Light into your life doesn't mean it's wrong to get pleasure from the sex act. On the contrary, it's perfectly natural to enjoy it. But in order to reveal the greatest Light in your relationship and in the world, the thought energy that goes into the act should be: *"I am giving Light and love to my beloved, and together we will create a circuit that will bring creative energy into the world."*

Even at the point of orgasm, look for more than just a flow of sexual fluid and the relief of muscular contraction; also expect an outpouring of love. This, of course, rules out casual sex, prostitution, and any form of sexuality that excludes love.

Am I saying that one should never seek out a one-night stand or experience different types of sexual relationships? You must be the judge of those activities and of their role in your life and your *tikune*. However, a relationship founded on spiritual principles is one in which the intention behind sexuality is to share Light with the world. When we do this, we automatically bring Light into our own lives, and our relationships as well as our lives thrive.

17

It's a God!
The Conception Tool

—

According to Kabbalah,

you chose your children and

your children chose you.

So far, I've been focusing on your relationship with your intimate partner. Most likely, this is the key relationship in your life as well as one
of the most important areas in which you can work on your correction.
However, many of the same principles that I've outlined throughout
the pages of this book also apply to your relationships with your children—relationships that are a big part of understanding who you are.
If you have no kids, you were certainly a child at one time, and so
much of what I am about to say will be relevant to you as well.

According to Kabbalah, you chose your children and your children
chose you. What do I mean by that? At the moment of conception,
your consciousness determines the kind of soul that will be drawn into
your baby's body. Prospective souls ready to come into this physical
world wait for the perfect moment, the perfect situation, and the
perfect environment to complete their *tikune*. They perceive the
thoughts and intentions of potential parents during the sex act and at
the moment of conception. These determine which soul chooses to
incarnate in your uterus.

Just as the apple seed contains all the information about the future
growth of that tree, the connection between parents at conception
paints an exact picture of what the soul will experience as their child.
Pretty powerful stuff, if you think about it.

Even for pure and holy people, the thoughts at the moment of conception determine everything. It is said that the reason Joseph is
referred to as Jacob's firstborn, even though Reuben was actually his

first son, is that on the night Jacob had relations with Leah, Laban tricked him. He thought he was sleeping with Rachel. Therefore, his *intention* was to have Joseph and not Reuben. Consequently, the title of firstborn was taken from Reuben and given to Joseph.

Imagine how important it must be for us—we who are not on the same spiritual plane as Jacob—to attend to our thoughts during sex. We don't have the spirituality needed to transcend the limits our thoughts may initially impose.

When you have sexual relations during your childbearing years, be aware that you might form a life. Be loving and sharing with your partner, and think of nothing but the relationship you are in. Concentrate your thoughts on the soul who may be coming into your union. If you can focus your energy on that level, your child will be conceived from the love of two people, and she will stand a better chance of being born into the Light.

Remember, there is no higher form of creation in this world than new life.

18

Have I Become My Mother?
The Parenting Tool

No contract is more important than
the one you have with your children.
No matter what you create or how large
your business grows, if you've lost touch
with your loved ones, you've neglected life
and traded it for something less.

If you approach the task of parenting in the right way, you can assist your children enormously in their spiritual work. You can also stimulate your own spiritual growth.

Child rearing begins when your baby is still in the womb. We know that when a pregnant woman drinks alcohol, smokes cigarettes, or takes drugs, toxins cross the placental barrier. Consequently, she is at greater risk of having a low-birth-weight or otherwise compromised baby than a woman who abstains.

The same is true of emotions. If you're resentful, spiteful, or angry while you're pregnant—if you're self-centered or otherwise uninvolved in elevating your consciousness, or if you're unkind or uncaring toward people around you—then you're also failing to nurture the life growing inside you.

How you relate to your baby's father is important as well. If your relationship includes the circuitry of love, then the child being formed in the womb will also enjoy wonderful energy. When parents-to-be create this kind of loving connection during the pregnancy, their baby is well nurtured. Love is the supreme food for the soul growing within. But if you fight with your partner and your child is conceived by accident, or if during the time of conception your thoughts were perhaps on others, then conflict will reside within this nascent soul.

The first few months are the most critical in your baby's life. Loads of cuddling and loving coupled with breast-feeding give your infant core feelings of safety that he will need to grow into a secure adult. Some people believe that very young children are hardly developed, but in fact their personalities are fully formed before their third birthdays. If you want your child to love the earth and all people, give him the security of your loving arms at the beginning, and it will pay off in spades later in life.

Children also need the space to express their own thoughts and make their own mistakes. When you tell your child that there is no "boogey-man"—if you tell him that he's just "seeing things" and send him back to sleep after he cries—you shrink his imagination and undermine his self-esteem. Instead, let him know that there are "good angels" who watch over all of us. Sometimes they frighten us because we don't know what they are. Create a little prayer with your children to welcome these wonderful forces into their lives. By doing so, you will encourage them to connect with the cosmic energies at play all around us.

Be clear about what you really want to give your offspring. I've raised four children in our home, and my main objective has always been to help them be who they are. Today, as adults, they all have great strength of character, wisdom, and deep values. They came to this place not from what I taught them, but from what they saw and experienced in our household.

This is an important point to understand. Children don't learn from being lectured to; they learn by seeing and doing. When you scream at your spouse, your child will take on that resentment and become an angry adult. If your child sees your husband express disrespect toward you or vice versa, he will become, in turn, a disrespectful adult. In either case, the Light will shine less strongly in his life.

The same applies when it comes to values. You don't want your children to go out on the streets and take drugs or try things that you know are dangerous for them. But are you setting the right example? Do you or your spouse pour a drink in order to unwind, and then turn to your child and admonish him not to smoke marijuana? If you don't restrict your own addictive tendencies, why should you expect your child to do so?

When my kids were growing up, one of my friends thought I was a terrible housewife. I didn't mind this much, since it was true. Sheila observed that I would let the children do whatever they wanted in my house, but whenever they were in someone else's home, they understood that they weren't allowed to make a mess or touch anything. They sat still like adults. "You're being a hypocrite," she chided.

"But my children behave this way," I explained, "not because I taught them to, but because they watched me act respectfully when I visited others. They understand from my example that you can do what you want with your own property, but you must have respect for someone else's."

The same applies to a quality such as generosity. A child whose parents are withholding and are constantly worried will have difficulty growing into a sharing person. If you want your youngsters to acquire certain values, make sure they witness those values in your home. Whatever you want them to be, focus on being that yourself. The rest will follow.

Also make time for your kids. If you work outside the home, be fully present with your children when you're with them. This means listening to their problems with interest and concern; hearing the emotion beneath their words; and empathizing with their feelings. If your children can't get the high that comes from receiving your contact and attention, they'll look for it elsewhere—potentially from peers who might provide the wrong kind of influence.

When my boys were growing up, the Rav and I had the good fortune to be with them day and night. We walked with them, played with them, told them stories and sang songs with them before they went to bed, and lay down to sleep with them. They are the people they are today, I think, mostly because of that—because they were nurtured. When you give that kind of love and appreciation to your child, you get it back in return. But if you don't have the time, or if you're too tired or bored, or if you're just plain absent, you can't expect your kids to grow up with a strong sense of self and purpose.

Isn't it interesting that we often find the most dysfunctional families in the most affluent homes? Somewhere along the way, priorities get lost. But a busy parent who takes at least a few hours a week to be alone with his youngsters at the local park or swimming pool, showing them how important they are to him, goes a long way toward raising emotionally healthy kids.

No contract is more important than the one you have with your children. No matter what you create or how large your business grows, if you've lost touch (literally) with your loved ones, you've neglected life and traded it for something less.

19

Have a Social Life:
The Friendship Tool

Friends don't judge each other.

Judgment is ego at work.

Once there was a man who humiliated the King. The monarch, in his anger, condemned Jonathan to death.

"Your Majesty," Jonathan pleaded with the King, "I know I'm to be executed, but please grant me three days to put my affairs in order."

The King was skeptical. "How can I know that you will return in three days?"

Andrew, Jonathan's best friend, then stepped from the crowd. "I'll take his place, Your Majesty." he volunteered. "I'll vouch for his return with my life."

"Okay," the King agreed, somewhat reluctantly. "If that's what you want." And Andrew was escorted to jail while Jonathan sped off to say his good-byes and finish his business.

At the end of the third day, as the time for the execution approached, Jonathan failed to appear. The guards ushered Andrew to the gallows. As the hangman placed the noose around his neck, a ruckus suddenly arose at the fringe of the crowd.

Jonathan came racing up, shouting, "Wait. Stop. I'm here. Don't kill the wrong man."

But Andrew, standing on the scaffold, became stubborn, and an argument ensued. "You didn't get here in time," he protested, "So I'm taking your place."

"No," Jonathan shouted in reply. "I committed the crime, and it's my punishment."

"You have a family," Andrew retorted, "and I don't. Go home to your children."

They carried on in this way until the King finally stepped in. "My friends," he said, "my decision had been to put only one man to death. But I see that if I carry out this judgment I will be killing two, not one. Executioner, remove the noose from Andrew's neck."

And so it was that the wise king let the two friends go free.

True friendship means you would take a bullet for someone else. It's a rare thing indeed. We use the word friendship lightly, but a person who has even one true friend in this life is greatly blessed.

Sadly, most friendships are superficial. Many people look for friends who agree with them, who share their political beliefs or cultural attitudes, or who party with them when times are good. But this is not true friendship. No, what these individuals are really doing is seeking support for the image of who they think they are and what they stand for. They're simply bolstering their own egos.

The ego is a fragile thing. Since it's not real, it needs support from others in order to be maintained. People surround themselves with friends to feel better about themselves and more secure in their opinions, but that has nothing to do with real friendship. Indeed, real friendship is never based on ego.

So how do you go about finding a true friend—someone for whom you would lay down your life, and who would lay down her life for you?

First, you have to know how to be alone. This will help you understand who you are. If you feel inadequate, that's what you'll bring to the relationship.

Second, look inside yourself to see what stops you from being a true friend to yourself and to others. You can't ask another person to be what you are not. To have a real friend, you must first be a real friend. This means setting your ego aside and caring unconditionally for another. Here is where acting like the Light and using the sharing tool come to the fore.

Third, examine your motives. In many friendships, each individual is seeking to get something from the other. You might not recognize this at first, but take a close look at what happens if your friend changes her behavior—if, for instance, she stops listening to your problems because she's going through a tough time herself. If you find yourself willing to end the relationship over a mere disagreement, this is obviously not a true friendship. Again, it's a question of whether you're stuck in a "me, me, me" mentality or whether you're willing to restrict your impulses and be sharing and proactive.

Fourth, ask yourself, "What kind of friends do I really want?" Once your consciousness starts to elevate, old friends may drift away, and your relationships with some or all of them may dissolve. Perhaps you enjoyed going to a bar with them on a Friday night to toss back a few beers—and, incidentally, there's nothing wrong with that—but now that your interests have grown, you prefer a spiritual gathering to the bar scene. You feel more fulfilled there. Your friends haven't changed, but you have. You now draw another level of person to you, someone with whom you can perhaps form a deeper, more meaningful connection.

* * *

In a real friendship, you always try to do what is best for the other person. This could mean letting her dominate the conversation (without feeling resentful) because she's really hurting and needs a shoulder to cry on. Or it could even mean disconnecting from her if you believe it's in her best interests.

One of my friends had been trying for five years to conceive. On the day I discovered I was pregnant with my first child, Debra called to share the great news that she too was expecting a baby. We became even closer during this exciting time. We used the same doctor and the same hospital, and we even planned to be together in the same room during delivery.

Debra went into labor first. But when her baby was born, the doctors discovered a severe birth defect.

Three days later, I went into labor.

Debra's daughter died at 9:00 A.M. that morning, and my daughter was born 30 minutes later.

Our husbands sat together in the waiting room when our doctor came out to break the news that their child had died, but that I had given birth to a healthy baby girl.

At first, no one told me what had happened. But when I found out, I called Debra. Understandably, she was devastated. I wanted to visit her, but she couldn't bear to be around me. "Look, Karen," she said to me, "I know you mean well, but I can't see you and your baby without being reminded of the death of my little Lisa. Not that I wish you harm or anything, but it's an open sore right now."

I wanted to help Debra, but it became clear to me that the best way to do this was to stay away from her so that I wouldn't cause her further pain.

You might think that this tragedy marked the end of our friendship, but in fact, it just deepened it. Today Debra has five healthy kids,—but at that time, she needed distance. That was what our friendship demanded, and happily, I was able to give it to her without taking her request personally and reacting to it.

* *, *

Every successful marriage, partnership, or relationship of any kind is based on friendship. A couple might live together as man and wife but have nothing in common. Sexual intimacy can keep two people together for only so long before they need something more. Common interests and goals are what bind a couple together as friends so that their relationship thrives.

Friendship means you can be part of someone else's life without injuring each other. You accept your partner. You know all about him and still like him.

Friends don't judge each other. Judgment is ego at work. Perhaps your partner likes to be silly in company. He enjoys joking and laughing, but you feel uncomfortable when he acts that way. Why? Is it because you believe his behavior reflects badly on you? Your real concern is how you look. That's ego, not love.

Knock gently on another's heart and be grateful for the chance to look inside. Love is respectful. Love means relating to your friend or lover while allowing him to be himself.

It is hard work getting to this elevated level of consciousness because it requires constant mindfulness. You must be vigilant. Notice how your ego always wants to control others. Then stop yourself from engaging in that behavior.

How do you know when you have a true friendship? I think it is when you can say these words to your friend, and mean them:

I love you not only for what you are

But for what I am when I am with you.

I love you not only for what you have made of yourself

But for what you are making of me.

I love you for putting your hand

Into my heaped-up heart

And passing over all the foolish weak things

That you cannot help but dimly see there,

And for bringing out into the light

All the beautiful belongings

That no one else had looked quite far enough to find,

For helping me to make out of the lumber of my life

Not a tavern but a temple,

Out of the works of my every day

Not a reproach but a song.

You have done more than any creed could have done

to make me good

And more than any faith could have done

To make me happy.

You have done this without a word, without a sign.

You have done it by being yourself.

That perhaps is what a friend is after all.

—Anonymous

20

Can You Hear Me Now?
The Prayer Tool

Take that special time at least once a week

to talk to the inner spark that is you,

and tell it all the things you want to do.

In this book we have talked about all kinds of relationships, but not necessarily about your relationship to God. So what is the link between you and the Creator? How do you make that connection? And what does it mean to pray?

As we have seen, Kabbalah tells us that the world doesn't exist on just what we can experience with our senses. There is a force beyond—a metaphysical source, the Light—that also motivates all the things we want from life.

We know that we have the Light inside ourselves. If we believe that all of our actions create reactions—if that's true—then we must understand that our relationship to the Light inside us is of primary importance. How do we draw down the right children? Why do some couples have difficulties with their parents? Why do others struggle with money or health? What causes one woman to cling to an abusive or neglectful man and another to feel unsatisfied even when her husband caters to her every whim? Where does happiness come from, and why don't we all bask in it?

A great deal has to do with karma. Despite our beliefs to the contrary, none of us control our own lives purely from the present time. Most of us come into our current bodies with lots of baggage and karma from our last life. Our job, our *tikune*, is to detach ourselves from the negative karma and put ourselves into a more positive place. And we call karma into our lives by the way we speak to our Creator—by the way we pray.

WHAT TO PRAY FOR

Prayer is just a way to acknowledge to the Creator that we understand we're not entitled to all the things we have—which includes the ability to acknowledge even this.

There is a story of a great sage who was hours late for a meeting. "Why?" his students asked. "Why were you so late?"

His reply: "I was standing before God and thanking God."

Most of us don't even consider that possibility. We feel everything is coming to us; we're entitled to walk, to talk, to see. We never say, "Thank you for the eyes that enable me to see this beautiful place and to read this book. Thank you for the ears to hear the music of my baby's voice. Thank you for my voice that sings of love." We take these many gifts for granted. But we do have the right to ask for things in prayer, and especially to create for ourselves a way to become a more spiritual being.

They say that of all the Gates of Heaven, the Gates of Tears are always open. But if they are unlocked, why do we need such a gate in the first place?

The answer is simple. If you go to God and cry that you're not as good as you should be, that you're a procrastinator and a gossip, that you want to be more humble, you lament because you recognize your frailties. And when you ask for help in becoming a better person, the Gates open. But the Gates close to your request if you sit there in the guise of prayer saying, "Becky has everything: a Mercedes, a big house, maids. I don't have any of those things. I'm so needy. Please allow me to be equal to her." That's why we need a gate.

So what do we pray for? The more we are aware, the less we think about others. We all have blessings in our lives even if we're losing money in the stock market, even if we fight with our kids, even if we fall into the negative—even when life seems so dark. So what do we pray for? *The ability to acknowledge that God is in everything.*

PRAYER AND KARMA

A young student comes to his teacher because he doesn't believe in the idea that there is fairness and justice in life. "How can you help me understand this?" he asks of his teacher.

"Go to the corner of Oak Street and Main," his teacher replies. "You'll find a bench there. Across the street is a tree. Sit under that tree and watch what happens on the bench."

The student thinks this answer is rather curious, but he decides to follow his teacher's instructions. So he finds the intersection and the tree. And just as he sits down to watch, a man approaches the bench. The man takes a seat and opens a brown paper bag. From it, he pulls not his lunch but a huge wad of $100 bills, which he proceeds to count very carefully. The man then puts the money back in the bag but gets distracted by the time. He checks his watch and acts as if he's late for a meeting. He rushes off, but forgets his bag with the money in it.

A second man arrives. He sits down and notices the brown paper bag. Opening it, his eyes grow wide as he spies the cash. He looks around furtively; no one is watching. So he stashes the bag under his coat and runs.

Now a third man arrives. He sits down to have his lunch. He opens his brown bag, pulls out a sandwich, and starts eating when the first guy returns in search of his lost cash. "Where's my bag? Where's my money?" he demands angrily.

"Look," fellow number three say, "I have no idea what you're talking about. I sat down here to eat my lunch. I don't know anything about any money. You can look for yourself."

But the first man is incensed. He beats the hapless fellow to a pulp.

The student sitting under the tree is now completely confused. He returns to his teacher and asks, "Where's the justice in this? I saw a man lose money he didn't deserve to lose; I saw a man find money he didn't deserve to find and get off scot-free; and I saw a man beaten for no reason at all. I just don't understand what you sent me to see and how this is going to prove that there is justice in the world."

To this the wise teacher replied, "We have to look to the last lives of these men to understand the justice in this situation. The first man and the second man were partners in this earlier incarnation. The first man had embezzled money from their business and had caused the second man great hardship. So the second man was only getting back what rightly belonged to him, while the first was getting what he deserved." "And the third man, the one who was beaten?" inquired the student. "Oh," continued the teacher, "he was the judge who let the first man go free."

We look at painful lifetime situations—a person born into a karma of abuse, a child born out of wedlock, a young man who is murdered in the prime of his life—and we ask, "The Creator, this all-merciful being, is good? How is this possible if innocents suffer?" But if we see that the soul inside the abused child perpetrated just such an act in a previous lifetime, it is possible to understand his painful situation today. The Light sent here in the form of a soul and the amount of energy that soul possesses will eventually go back to the Creator. And one hopes that soul will have learned its lesson and will incarnate, removing a certain amount of the negative karma in a future life.

We are born in a specific place to specific parents. We are given this environment to nurture our ability to change the karma of the last lifetime. How can we change our karma? Sometimes when we connect to the Source by praying, we can sway the way life presents itself to us.

The Zohar tells us that three things are not in our power: life; the number of children we will have; and the amount of money we will make. These are predetermined and depend on Mazal. But there are many discussions in *The Bible* of what happens when we try to motivate forces. *The Bible* tells us about Hannah, for instance, who desperately wanted a baby. She went to a festival on Mount Moriah. The high priest Eli thought she'd had too much wine because of the way she closed her eyes, swayed, and moved her lips.

"How dare you come to such a holy place drunk." he chided her.

"I'm just begging God with all of my might for a child," she replied. And lo and behold, with the passage of time, Hannah gave birth to the prophet Samuel. After she weaned him, she gave him to the Prophets to raise as one of their own.

King David knew that he was to die on a Saturday night, but he didn't know which Saturday night. So every Saturday night that passed during which he didn't die, he threw a party called *Malavah Malka*—a farewell to the Shabbat queen. Even though someone has a determinate time at the end, he can still alter the outcome.

Life is a game. We're challenged by the game in relationships and in partnerships. If we always fall for the negativity of the challenge, the time we're allotted is sometimes shortened. We can lose time, and our lives grow shorter. So every Saturday King David lived, he celebrated that God had given him extra time.

We may give birth to a child who has been ordained to become a thief. This can mean a little kid who runs to the store to steal a candy bar, or it can be a bank robber on the order of Bonnie and Clyde. What determines the amount of negativity? The connection we have with the Light Force and karma, which can be altered by our behavior—by the good deeds we do and how we relate each day with other people.

The connection we have with God in our lives must be acknowledged all the time, not just in times of need. When we create a negative space in our lives, we lose for that period of time all the good we've done. Why should the Creator answer us? Just because we need something? "You've got so much on loan already," God says. "I don't know if your request warrants another advance."

HOW TO PRAY

Most of us should take at least 20 minutes of quiet time to pray. If you choose to, you can burn a candle and sit in a quiet room; you can watch clouds; or you can just walk the dog. Take that special time at least once a week to talk to the inner spark that is you, and tell it all the things you want to do. Acknowledge that there are situations you can control and others that are presented to you to give you a message. The most difficult part is to understand what you need to change. Like me, you may think you're perfect.

This is one form of prayer. But there is another—when your faith is tested. We live in a world in which we are given choices or cassettes in life. If we take a certain road, we get one cassette. If we go another way, we get a different cassette. The choice of cassette is up to us. God does not punish. It is by our choices that we are punished. In the 99% world, everything is perfect. A man may be whole even if he has lost a leg. A woman may be whole even if she is unable to bear a child she so desperately wants.

Let us pray that by our acts of kindness, by our desire to receive for the sake of sharing, we move ourselves closer to that more perfect place. We women are already created as higher spiritual Vessels. May we use that Vessel to further all that is good and sweet in life, now and always.

EPILOGUE

Now that you've read *God Wears Lipstick*, you may agree with much of what I said. You may understand a woman's dual role as Vessel as well as Light. You may see quite readily that tolerance, respect, and taking responsibility are necessary ingredients for a successful relationship. You might have begun to understand the importance of circuitry in a relationship, and you may now appreciate that unconditional sharing brings Light, which is love, into your life. You may realize that this circuitry is created when you restrict your reactive nature—your ego—and allow consciousness to enter. This is the "circuitry of love."

I hope some of these concepts have indeed become clear to you, but I must warn you that more than intellectual understanding is required. Vigilance and sincerity are needed if you are to make lasting change. You must want, above all other things, to bring the Light into your life and your relationships, and you must be ever vigilant so that you can see when your old reactive nature is taking charge again.

Keep dipping back into this book so that you stay in contact with the principles and tools I've presented here. Try to associate with like-minded people who are on the same path as you and will encourage you. Become involved in a spiritual organization—it could be The Kabbalah Centre or any other place that feels right to you—so that you stay close to people who are bringing Light into the world.

Above all, be patient and kind with yourself. You are in this world to learn, so start by learning to enjoy the process.

More books that can help you bring the wisdom of Kabbalah into your life

The Prayer of the Kabbalist: The 42 - Letter Name of God
By Yehuda Berg

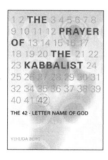

According to the ancient wisdom of Kabbalah, the powerful prayer known as *Ana Bekho'ah* invokes The 42-Letter Name of God, which connects to no less than the undiluted force of creation. By tapping into this connection through the Prayer, you can leave the past behind and make a fresh start. If you recite the Prayer on a regular basis, you are able to use the force of creation to create miracles, both in your everyday life and in the world at large. This book explains the meaning behind the 42 letters and gives you practical steps for how best to connect to their power.

The Power of Kabbalah
By Yehuda Berg

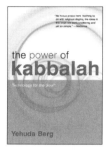

Imagine your life filled with unending joy, purpose, and contentment. Imagine your days infused with pure insight and energy. This is *The Power of Kabbalah*. It is the path from the momentary pleasure that most of us settle for, to the lasting fulfillment that is yours to claim. Your deepest desires are waiting to be realized. Find out how, in this basic introduction to the ancient wisdom of Kabbalah.

The Secret: Unlocking the Source of Joy & Fulfillment
By Michael Berg

The Secret reveals the essence of life in its most concise and powerful form. Several years before the latest "Secret" phenomenon, Michael Berg shared the amazing truths of the world's oldest spiritual wisdom in this book. In it, he has pieced together an ancient puzzle to show that our common understanding of life's purpose is actually backwards, and that anything less than complete joy and fulfillment can be changed by correcting this misperception.

Immortality: The Inevitability of Eternal Life
By Rav Berg

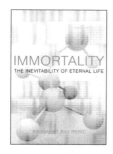

This book will totally change the way in which you perceive the world, if you simply approach its contents with an open mind and an open heart.

Most people have it backwards, dreading and battling what they see as the inevitability of aging and death. But, according to the great Kabbalist Rav Berg and the ancient wisdom of Kabbalah, it is eternal life that is inevitable.

With a radical shift in our cosmic awareness and the transformation of the collective consciousness that will follow, we can bring about the demise of the death force once and for all—in this "lifetime."

Secrets of the Zohar: Stories and Meditations to Awaken the Heart
By Michael Berg

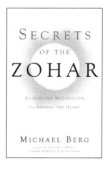

The *Zohar*'s secrets are the secrets of the Bible, passed on as oral tradition and then recorded as a sacred text that remained hidden for thousands of years. They have never been revealed quite as they are here in these pages, which decipher the codes behind the best stories of the ancient sages and offer a special meditation for each one. Entire portions of the *Zohar* are presented, with the Aramaic and its English translation in side-by-side columns. This allows you to scan and to read aloud so that you can draw on the *Zohar*'s full energy and achieve spiritual transformation. Open this book and open your heart to the Light of the *Zohar*!

Wheels of a Soul
By Rav Berg

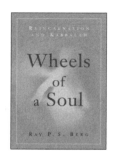

In *Wheels of a Soul*, Kabbalist Rav Berg explains why we must acknowledge and explore the lives we have already lived in order to understand the life we are living today. Make no mistake: You have been here before. Just as science is now beginning to recognize that time and space may be nothing but illusions, Rav Berg shows why death itself is the greatest illusion of all.

Angel Intelligence
By Yehuda Berg

Discover how billions of angels exist and shape the world, and how, through your thoughts and deeds, you have the power to create them, whether positive or negative. You'll learn their individual names and characteristics and their unique roles, as well as how to call on them for different purposes and use them as powerful spiritual tools for transformation. By becoming aware of the angel dynamics at work in the universe and by learning how to connect with these unseen energy forces, you will gain amazing insight and the ability to meet life's greatest challenges.

God Wears Lipstick Card Deck
By Karen Berg

The Zohar

"**Bringing *The Zohar* from near oblivion to wide accessibility has taken many decades. It is an achievement of which we are truly proud and grateful.**"

—Michael Berg

Composed more than 2,000 years ago, *The Zohar* is a set of 23 books, a commentary on biblical and spiritual matters in the form of conversations among spiritual masters. But to describe *The Zohar* only in physical terms is greatly misleading. In truth, *The Zohar* is nothing less than a powerful tool for achieving the most important purposes of our lives. It was given to all humankind by the Creator to bring us protection, to connect us with the Creator's Light, and ultimately to fulfill our birthright of true spiritual transformation.

Eighty years ago, when The Kabbalah Centre was founded, *The Zohar* had virtually disappeared from the world. Few people in the general population had ever heard of it. Whoever sought to read it—in any country, in any language, at any price—faced a long and futile search. Today all this has changed. Through the work of The Kabbalah Centre and the editorial efforts of Michael Berg, *The Zohar* is now being brought to the world, not only in the original Aramaic language but also in English.

The new English Zohar provides everything for connecting to this sacred text on all levels: the original Aramaic text for scanning; an English translation; and clear, concise commentary for study and learning.

The Kabbalah Centre

The International Leader in the Education of Kabbalah

Since its founding, The Kabbalah Centre has had a single mission: to improve and transform people's lives by bringing the power and wisdom of Kabbalah to all who wish to partake of it.

Through the lifelong efforts of Rav Berg, his wife Karen, and the great spiritual lineage of which they are a part, an astonishing 3.5 million people around the world have already been touched by the powerful teachings of Kabbalah. And each year, the numbers are growing!

As the leading source of kabbalistic wisdom with 50 locations around the world, The Kabbalah Centre offers you a wealth of resources, including:

- The English *Zohar*, the first-ever comprehensive English translation of the foundation of kabbalistic wisdom. In 23 beautifully bound volumes, this edition includes the full Aramaic text, the English translation, and detailed commentary, making this once-inaccessible text understandable to all.

- A full schedule of workshops, lectures, and evening classes for students at all levels of knowledge and experience.

- CDs, audiotapes, videotapes, and books in English and ten other languages.

- One of the Internet's most exciting and comprehensive websites, www.kabbalah.com—which receives more than 100,000 visitors each month.

- A constantly expanding list of events and publications to help you live the teachings of Kabbalah with greater understanding and excitement.

Discover why The Kabbalah Centre is one of the world's fastest-growing spiritual organizations. Our sole purpose is to improve people's lives through the teachings of Kabbalah. Let us show you what Kabbalah can do for you!

Each Kabbalah Centre location hosts free introductory lectures. For more information on Kabbalah or on these and other products and services, call 1-800-KABBALAH.

Wherever you are, there's a Kabbalah Centre—because now you can call 1-800-KABBALAH from almost anywhere, 18 hours a day, and get answers or guidance right over the telephone. You'll be connected to distinguished senior faculty who are on hand to help you understand Kabbalah as deeply as you want to—whether it involves recommending a course of study; deciding which books/tapes to take or the order in which to take them; discussing the material; or anything else you wish to know about Kabbalah.

May ALL find true and lasting happiness.

May ALL be free from suffering.

May ALL find true and lasting peace.

To my parents, my first teachers, my wife Sarah, my second teacher and all those who have walked together with us since 1982 and held us in this sacred chalice of a blessed marriage,

I wish sublime healing, unending love and irrepressible joy.

–Alex Nimick